PERSONAL FINANCE FOR TEENS AND YOUNG ADULTS

FINANCIAL LITERACY SKILLS TO EMPOWER YOUR FUTURE, CRUSH YOUR DEBT, AND BUILD SMART MONEY HABITS THAT INSTILL LIFELONG CONFIDENCE

GEORGIA I. LAINIOTIS, MBA, MA

EMPOWER YOUR FINANCIAL FUTURE TODAY!

Welcome to a journey of financial empowerment with "Personal Finance for Teens and Young Adults"! This book is your gateway to understanding and conquering the financial world.

Join PersonalFinance4Teens Today!
Special Offer for Aspiring Financial Whizzes!

Join the PersonalFinance4Teens Community today and receive an exclusive, FREE guide: "Top 21 Teen Banking Apps: Your Gateway to Financial Freedom." This isn't just a list; it's the beginning of your journey to financial independence.

What You'll Discover:

- **Effortless Budgeting Techniques**: Learn to navigate your finances with ease and confidence.
- **Debt-Busting Strategies**: Equip yourself with tools to overcome financial hurdles.
- **Investment Wisdom for Beginners**: Start building your wealth with informed decisions.

Start Your Path to Financial Freedom Today – Join Us and Transform Your Tomorrow!

Take Action Now

Join Now! Scan the QR Code Below

Embrace this opportunity to gain essential financial skills and knowledge. Join us and take an important step towards shaping your **successful financial future!**

CONTENTS

INTRODUCTION

Money speaks the language of your mindset.

— ARYAN CHAUDHARY

There has never been a better time to learn about personal finance than now. With advancements in technology and the world evolving at a fast pace, keeping up with the latest financial trends and learning ways to improve your finances is a must. Gone are the days when the subject of money was mainly discussed by working-class people. Nowadays, the internet is filled with inspiring stories of young folks who have built businesses from their college dorms with nothing but an idea, an internet connection, and a computer. For example, you have probably read an article or two about how Mark Zuckerberg started Facebook in his Harvard dorm room at the age of 19. Today, Facebook is worth $320 billion, and is the fastest-growing social media platform in the world (Reynolds, 2023).

ALMOST ANYTHING IS POSSIBLE

There are many other young entrepreneurs who have made a name for themselves in business, such as 17–year–old Evan Moana, who founded his *EvanTubeHD* YouTube channel when he was only in the fourth grade, and became YouTube's youngest millionaire in 2016. His first YouTube videos were reviews of popular children's toys, and since then, Moana's YouTube channel has grown to over seven million subscribers (Post, 2023), with over 900 videos showcasing toys and gadgets as well as science experiments and food challenges he does with his sister Jillian.

Nineteen-year-old Maya Penn, CEO of Maya's Ideas, is another example of how an idea can give birth to a million-dollar business empire. Penn founded her company, which produces fashion accessories, when she was just 8 years old. She is not only the CEO and designer of her company, but she is also an environmental activist, speaker, and author of the book, *You Got This! Unleash Your Awesomeness, Find Your Path and Change the World*. In 2011, at age 11, Penn founded Maya's Ideas for The Planet, a non-profit organization that distributes sanitary products to women in developing countries.

HOW I CAN HELP

Maybe you are wondering, *How can I save up cash for my college fund?* Or, perhaps like these young entrepreneurs, you are wondering how you can make an impact in the world and get financial rewards for it.

Research showed that 75% of teenagers in America do not have confidence in their knowledge of personal finance (Turner, 2023). In the same study, adults were asked what parts of personal finance they worried about most. A significant 17% of them said they worried about not having enough for retirement (Turner, 2023). These statistics alone should inspire young people to learn about personal finance and prepare for their financial future.

The subject of personal finance is broad; there is no one-size-fits-all advice I can give. What works for one person may not work for the other. However, the basic rules of money are the same, and they apply to everyone who is looking to build wealth over the long term.

I remember my first earnings. I was 13, and I asked my father to buy me a new watch. Even though I did not need one, my father said if I wanted a watch, I had to work for it. So, he found me a job at one of his work conferences as a tour operator assistant. I earned my first $100 from that job.

From that experience, I learned the concept of working for money, and because I understood how difficult it was to work for money, I decided not to buy the watch and save the money instead. This was an important lesson about delayed gratification for me.

From then on, I decided to develop my skills and build my experience by enrolling in internships. My goal was to gain as much work experience as I could by the time I graduated from college. After graduation, I had no trouble landing my first paid internship at Morgan Stanley.

Since then, I have worked in various companies in the finance sector. I founded a fintech company, which I sold five years later. I have also coached many teenagers and young adults over the course of my career, helping them to acquire internships. I have helped many young people set up businesses, get financial aid, change colleges to save money and pay off debt, and to build their resumes. Some of the young people I have coached have become quite successful, and most of them came from families that could not afford to support them financially.

My passion lies in helping teenagers and young adults understand finances, the new job market, and the importance of choosing the right path in life. I believe that with the right tools and knowledge, anyone can be successful. Financial literacy plays a key role in your quality of life. Without learning money management skills, it is easy to fall into the financial pitfalls most people find themselves in.

PLANNING FOR THE FUTURE AND BUILDING WEALTH

We live in a world with so much uncertainty. The COVID-19 pandemic is an example of how certain events can hit you unexpectedly in life, and if you are not financially prepared to weather the storm, this can negatively impact your finances.

Because of the economic impact the pandemic had, some companies had to close down, while others downsized, leaving many people without their primary source of income. This not only affected individuals, it affected entire families who were used to a certain lifestyle.

How best can you prepare yourself for such unexpected events? If you are just starting to learn about personal finance and looking for a simplified way to learn financial literacy, I wrote this book with you in mind. My goal is to help teenagers and young adults gain financial freedom so they can make a difference in their families and communities. If you want to get ahead fast in life, learn financial literacy. The earlier you start managing your finances, the better your chances are of having a bright financial future.

Building wealth involves learning and applying the rules of money. It is about developing the right money mindset and discipline to create and stick to a financial plan. It is understanding the importance of creating a monthly budget, how it can help you keep track of your finances, and how it can prevent financial leakages.

Building wealth means understanding the financial system and how it can help you make informed decisions about your finances. Throughout this book, you will learn the money habits that wealthy people use to generate income. You will also learn how to develop the right money mindset and prepare for your financial future.

1

THE MILLIONAIRE MINDSET—IT IS NOT WHAT YOU THINK

Learn to control your money so it does not control you. When money is your best friend and not your biggest fear— then you are on the path to becoming financially free!

— GEORGIA I LAINIOTIS

What is the distinguishing factor between people who have amassed wealth and those who live paycheck to paycheck? Some people would say luck plays a role in the success of the wealthy. Others could argue it is because successful people come from wealthy families and had a good head start in life, unlike those who came from families who struggled financially. Well, while there are many factors that lead to financial success, there is one common factor that successful people share: their mindset.

Wealthy people think and do things differently. Millionaires allocate their time differently. They spend their time and money on personal development, investments, and mentors who teach them the secrets to building wealth. They create strategies for saving and investing and understand the importance of creating multiple sources of income.

Managing your money is as much about your mindset as it is about the opportunities that present themselves in your life. We have all heard the advice, "To manage your money well, live below your means and invest in your future." While this is good financial advice, it often leaves most people with the question of how one lives below their means when the money they earn is not enough to cover even a minor financial emergency.

An article published by CNBC revealed that 40% of Americans would struggle to settle an unexpected $400 bill (Nova, 2019). In another study, researchers found that 60% of U.S. adults had debit and credit card debt (Turner, 2023). The same study revealed that in 2020, about 4% of U.S. adults fell victim to some form of financial fraud. These statistics clearly show that there is a need for financial literacy to be taught in schools, from a young age. Families must talk more about money-related issues and not only address the subject when they are faced with a crisis.

If you are starting out in life, perhaps you have just landed your first job, or you are still in school and would like to avoid some of the financial mistakes most people make, the question on your mind right now could be, *What can I do to get different results?*

Managing your money is more than just punching figures on a calculator. It requires a different mindset. So, what does a millionaire mindset look like?

THE MILLIONAIRE MINDSET

What is it that separates millionaires apart from everyone else? Wealthy people commit to a savings plan, they have a budget, and tend to spend less. Spending more than you earn is a recipe for financial disaster, which has led many people to live from paycheck to paycheck and become slaves to money.

Here are a few factors that separate a millionaire mindset from a scarcity mindset.

- Successful people understand the importance of saving their money. With the recent rise in the cost of living, it is important not only to make money, but to save it in case of unexpected life events. A savings plan is personal—it depends on your financial obligations, the income you earn, your age, and your financial goals.
- Millionaires know how to grow their money and have it work for them. They have developed the discipline to spend less and live below their means.
- Wealthy people have multiple sources of income. This enables them to grow their net worth and come up with new, creative ideas to earn more money.
- Successful people invest in real estate and low-cost index funds. They spend their time learning about investments, and because they are financially literate,

they are risk tolerant and focus on their long-term financial goals.

- Wealthy people invest in their personal development. They spend the early hours of their mornings reading books and biographies of successful people to improve their mindset and develop habits of success.
- Rich people spend less time sleeping and more time thinking and brainstorming ideas to keep improving their lives.
- Those with wealth are consistent in their approach to financial matters. By doing the same things over and over, they have mastered what works for them and what does not. Consistency has led them to be masters in their fields of expertise.

UNDERSTANDING YOUR MONEY MINDSET

What are some of your beliefs about money? Do you believe that money is a scarce resource? Or, do you believe that there are plenty of opportunities for everyone to make money, and no one is an exception? Your beliefs about money influence your decisions and how you manage your finances. In simple terms, a money mindset is a set of beliefs you hold about money and how money impacts the world around you. Your attitude about money influences what you believe you are worthy of earning, what you can and cannot do with money, how much you give, where you invest your money, and how you utilize debt.

Your beliefs about money influence how you think about rich people and those living in poverty. Some people believe that rich people are evil, and that they use and manipulate the poor to keep amassing their wealth. Others believe that money is the root of evil and that being poor means being noble. The truth is, there is nothing noble about not having the financial means to support yourself. Money allows you to do good for your family, in your community, and in the world.

The way you feel about the subject of money is also a sign of your money mindset. Do you feel intimidated when talking about money, or you are confident enough to ask questions so you can learn more about finances?

The thing with your beliefs about money is that they exist at a subconscious level. Some of these beliefs formed when you were young, through the information you received at home from your parents, caregivers, friends, and close relatives. An awareness of your thoughts, feelings, and reactions toward money can help you understand your money mindset. You can then start working toward changing these beliefs and replacing them with new beliefs that support the future you are creating for yourself.

How a Money Mindset Is Formed

Most of your beliefs about money were formed when you were young, from observing and receiving information about money from the people you grew up with. Children do not have the experience or ability to choose what to believe or not to believe. Their tiny brains take everything fed to them as truth. Growing up, you probably observed how your parents, caregivers, friends, family members, and some of your community members dealt with money. That information formed your beliefs about money and influences your current decisions about saving, spending, and managing your finances.

Take a moment to reflect on the following questions. Reflecting on these questions will help you understand where your beliefs about money stem from.

- How is the subject of money handled in your family?
- Do your parents feel confident and calm when talking about money, or do they argue and blame each other for their financial struggles?

Your money mindset matters because it influences your behavior and attitude toward money. If you believe you can be successful, you'll do the things that bring success and wealth. If you believe that money is scarce and hard to come by, you'll create more of that belief in your life and live in scarcity.

ABUNDANCE VS. SCARCITY MINDSET

There's no doubt that most people want to get ahead in life. The fear of poverty drives most people to work tirelessly so they can earn more money. But, why is it that only a select few people have managed to build wealth while the rest are either broke or just getting by? The answer is simply that wealthy people have developed an abundance mindset that helps them spot opportunities instead of focusing on obstacles.

It's unfortunate that some people are born into families that are struggling financially. Growing up in an environment of poverty and lack instills the belief that there's not enough money in the world for everybody. Children who are born in homes facing financial hardships tend to develop a scarcity mindset. Growing up in an environment of lack reinforces negative beliefs about money. On the other hand, children born into families with financial stability often develop an abundance mindset. They believe in their abilities and limitless possibilities to make money. This mindset drives their behavior and allows them to achieve great success in life.

Characteristics of a Scarcity Mindset

A scarcity mindset leads most people to think there's not enough money and resources. This belief causes them to live in fear of not having enough money to get by. Following are a few signs of a scarcity mindset.

- Believing that you cannot change your circumstances and that they are permanent.
- Being afraid of change and not adapting new ways of thinking or doing things that will bring different results.
- A lack of motivation to learn and grow because you believe you already know it all. Financial literacy involves constant learning because financial trends are always changing. To improve your finances, you need to keep learning new ways to earn and invest your money.
- Envying other people's success. This often results in competitiveness. It builds resentment in you and makes it difficult for you to practice gratitude for what you already have.
- Negative self-talk and not believing in your abilities. Saying things such as, "I am not educated enough," or "I cannot do this" can cause you to let opportunities pass you by.
- Procrastination. When you procrastinate because you feel you are not qualified enough for an opportunity or you are somehow limited by your financial background, you will not take the risks that could potentially pay off and lead to financial success.

Characteristics of an Abundance Mindset

An abundance mindset, on the other hand, believes in limitless possibilities and that there are plenty of opportunities and resources for everyone. When you adopt an abundance mindset, you take control of your life and your finances. You become optimistic about what you are working to achieve and see opportunities where others see obstacles.

Signs of an abundance mindset include the following.

- Recognizing that no situation is permanent and that you can change your financial situation.
- Knowing the importance of asking for help when you need it.
- Understanding that small actions add up with time to produce massive results.
- Having a positive mindset and being excited by change and opportunities for growth.
- Being able to think long-term and see things from different perspectives.
- Being grateful and appreciating all the small pleasures of life. Gratitude can help you see things in a positive light even when you are going through a tough time.
- Practicing positive self-talk and having an "I can do this" attitude.
- Celebrating other people's success and recognizing that we all have an equal chance of achieving success

in life if we put in the effort and do the things that bring success and wealth.

- Being proactive rather than being reactive to what happens to you in life.
- Having a generous heart that shares time and resources instead of hoarding them.

An abundance mindset allows you to approach life positively. When you think positively you can turn obstacles into opportunities to learn and grow in your personal finance journey.

The Importance of Having an Abundance Mindset

An abundance mindset is important in every aspect of your life. It can help you build healthy relationships and it allows you to see the world as an abundant place. It makes you see endless possibilities where others see lack.

The one thing that keeps most people financially stuck is the fear of not having enough money in the future. This keeps them from investing money in fear of losing it. An abundance mindset understands that the world is a plentiful place and there will always be plenty of resources to go around.

An abundance mindset enables you to give with an open heart. Wealthy people are givers. They share their time, knowledge, and resources for the betterment of this world. This is because they believe that there are plenty of opportunities to make money, and they continue to create and develop new ideas that generate more income. Giving is a universal law; learning to apply this law can help you cultivate an abundance mindset.

Other benefits of developing an abundance mindset include the following.

- Learning to be flexible to change and understanding that life changes bring different opportunities to learn and grow.
- Helping you develop your problem-solving skills. An abundance mindset allows you to look for solutions when you face challenges and not play the victim.
- An abundance mindset opens you up to learning and developing yourself. You take responsibility for your financial future and devise strategies to improve your finances. You become intentional about what you do because you understand that your financial future depends on what you do today.

How to Develop an Abundance Mindset

If over the years you developed negative beliefs about money, you must change those beliefs and cultivate a more positive attitude toward finances. The good news is, mindset, like any other habit, can be changed.

It takes great effort and willpower to change negative beliefs, especially if you are unaware of them. At first, this may seem like a daunting task, but it will completely transform the way you think about money. To start cultivating an abundance mindset, try the following strategies.

Start With Awareness

You cannot solve a problem if you don't know what the problem is. To start cultivating an abundance mindset, you must first understand your limiting beliefs and how they are affecting your financial decisions. Pay attention to your thoughts, behaviors, and reactions toward money. Your thoughts about money influence your feelings, and your feelings in turn drive your behavior. For example, if you think that money is a scarce resource, you'll live in fear of losing it. Instead of being generous and sharing your resources, you'll hoard every dollar you earn because of the fear of not having enough money. On the other hand, developing an abundance mindset allows you to be generous. The more you help others, the more opportunities open up that will help you grow your finances.

Define What Abundance Means to You

Having a clear picture of what abundance looks like for you is important in helping you set your financial goals. To define abundance for yourself, take some time to reflect and answer the following questions.

- Does abundance mean time and money freedom to you?
- If you had more money what would you do?

- Where would you live?
- Where would you go?
- Does the thought of having more money make you feel empowered to help others, or does it make you happy and want to make more money for yourself?
- How much is enough money for you?

Create a Realistic Budget

Most people find it difficult to set and stick to a budget. Perhaps it is lacking an understanding of what a budget is and its purpose in financial management. A budget is a financial tool that helps you keep track of finances. It helps you understand how much you are earning and how much you are spending based on your lifestyle and spending habits.

Budgeting can help you create a long-term financial roadmap. It gives you insight into how much you earn and your monthly expenses, such as study materials, a cell phone bill, commuting or car expenses, food, and rent for your apartment or student accommodation.

Set Personal Goals

Setting personal goals can improve your overall well-being. Waking up each morning looking forward to achieving a worthy goal inspires creativity. It can help you build resilience when you are faced with challenges and enable you to stick to your plan until your goals are met.

To set achievable goals, ensure that your goals are SMART.

- **Specific:** Setting a specific and well-defined goal creates a clear vision of what you are working toward.
- **Measurable:** A measurable goal allows you to measure your progress and see if you are getting ahead or if you need to put in more effort.
- **Attainable:** Setting goals that are unattainable can cause you to lose the inspiration to work toward achieving them.
- **Realistic:** To achieve your goals, they must be realistic and within your abilities.
- **Time-bound:** Set a timeline for when you would like to achieve your goal. This will help you measure your progress and give you a necessary sense of urgency.

Save Money

One of the most effective ways to create an abundance mindset is by having money saved. It's difficult to feel grateful when you're broke and unable to afford your lifestyle.

When it comes to savings, small steps add up with time. The amount you decide to save is up to you and depends on your personal goals and earnings. Start with what you can afford to save. Review your budget from time to time to see if you can make adjustments to your spending and channel more funds into your savings.

Focus on Growth

Often, people with a scarcity mindset tend to have a rigid mindset. It's hard to learn anything new if you're closed-minded. An abundance mindset allows you to find solutions to problems. It allows you to brainstorm ideas on how to make money and reach your financial goals.

When faced with a difficult situation, ask yourself the following questions.

- What can I learn from this situation?
- How can I improve myself so that I get different results?
- What skills do I need to develop?
- How can I apply what I have learned from this situation in the future?

Use Positive Affirmations

You'd be amazed at how positive self-talk can help you think and feel optimistic about life. Positive self-talk is about reprogramming your mind to think in line with the future you are creating. If you do not reprogram your mind from past conditioning, your old limiting beliefs will continue sabotaging your relationship with money. So, to change those limiting beliefs, use positive affirmations such as:

- I am worthy of success.
- I deserve all the good things life has to offer; I deserve success.
- Abundance is my birthright. There are plenty of resources for all of us.
- I have everything I need.
- Money is easily drawn to me because I have a good relationship with my finances.

The power of affirmations lies in constant repetition. The more you say them to yourself, the more you start to believe them. This is how you change negative beliefs to positive ones.

To develop an abundance mindset, be grateful for what you have already. When you are grateful, you cultivate a positive attitude toward life and attract more circumstances to be grateful for.

At first, learning to manage your finances can feel like climbing a mountain. But, you do not have to do it alone. Ask your parents for some advice and seek a financial expert if you have to. A financial expert can help you learn more about personal finance and how you can prepare for your financial future. Speaking to a financial advisor can also help you decide what investment strategies you can employ that can help you grow your money based on your risk appetite, and they can also help you set your short and long-term financial goals.

WHAT IS YOUR MONEY PERSONALITY?

We approach money in four ways: worship, avoidance, vigilance, and status. Identifying your money personality can help you understand your money beliefs. Knowing what drives your financial decisions can help you build a healthier relationship with money.

Money Worshiper

Money worshippers believe money can solve all of their problems. They believe that money makes them powerful and happy.

Money Avoider

Money avoiders believe that money is bad, that wealthy people are greedy and manipulative, and that they take from the poor.

Money Vigilance

People who are vigilant have a healthy concern about saving money for emergencies and can be secretive about how much they earn.

Money Status

People who focus on money status believe their worth is tied to how much money they have or make. They believe in buying high-value brands and spending money to keep up with their lifestyle.

So, what's your money personality? To help you understand your current money mindset, take the following money personality quiz.

Money Personality Quiz

1. Life would be different if you had more money.

    a. Strongly agree
    b. Agree
    c. Agree a little
    d. Disagree a little
    e. Disagree
    f Strongly disagree

2. The more money you have, the happier you will be.

    a. Strongly agree
    b. Agree
    c. Agree a little
    d. Disagree a little
    e. Disagree
    f. Strongly disagree

3. Never disclose your earnings to anyone.

    a. Strongly agree
    b. Agree
    c. Agree a little

d. Disagree a little

e. Disagree

f. Strongly disagree

4. It is wrong to ask someone how much they earn.

a. Strongly agree

b. Agree

c. Agree a little

d. Disagree a little

e. Disagree

f. Strongly disagree

5. Most poor people do not deserve to have money.

a. Strongly agree

b. Agree

c. Agree a little

d. Disagree a little

e. Disagree

f. Strongly disagree

6. Wealthy people are greedy.

a. Strongly agree

b. Agree

c. Agree a little

d. Disagree a little

e. Disagree

f. Strongly disagree

7. You can either have money or love, but not both.

a. Strongly agree

b. Agree

c. Agree a little

d. Disagree a little

e. Disagree

f. Strongly disagree

Having more money when others have less than you is wrong.

a. Strongly agree

b. Agree

c. Agree a little

d. Disagree a little

e. Disagree

f. Strongly disagree

As you grow on your personal finance journey, refer to your answers to this money personality quiz from time to time to track your progress. The more you see positive changes, the more inspired you'll be to keep implementing the strategies and ideas outlined in this book to improve your finances.

Wealthy people have an abundance mindset which keeps them focused on what they can do instead of on their limitations. As you embark on this journey of building wealth, you must identify your limiting beliefs, let go of them, and adopt an abundance mindset, instead. An abundance mindset enables you to be proactive and take initiative toward securing your financial future.

Now that you've learned the importance of developing an abundance mindset in your personal finance journey, let's explore ways in which you can monetize your skills.

2

PASSION TO PROFIT

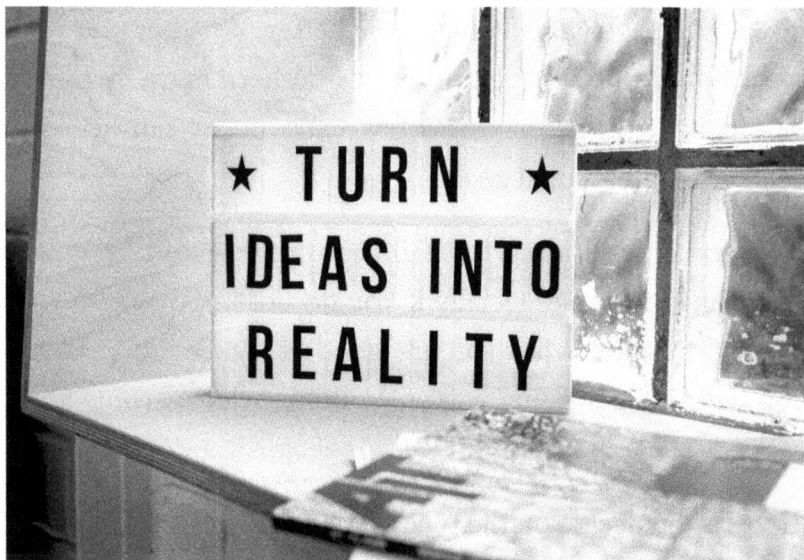

Create from the heart, for nature rewards a person, not for the thing he wants to profit from, but for that which he does for fun.

— MICHAEL BASSEY JOHNSON

C an one start making money at the age of 14? If yes, then what kind of work can a 14-year-old do? Fourteen years is a good time to start making your own money and learning more about personal finance. The earlier you start learning ways to earn and save money, and how to manage your finances, the better. Whether you want to save for your college tuition or you need extra cash for a new pair of kicks, making a few extra bucks can help you achieve your personal goals.

As a teenager, finding the right job for you can be a little confusing at first, especially if you do not know where your passion lies and what you are good at. But, with research, you will find a job that you enjoy doing while earning some cash.

To help you decide on the type of job to search for, first identify your current skills. What are you good at? Are you a creative genius and enjoy adding art to your work? You could come up with your own fashion design company—like the

Martinez brothers, Brandon (15) and Sebastian (13), founders of AreYouKidding Socks. The Martinez brothers design and sell colorful, stylish socks to enhance people's style while at the same time making a difference in society by donating some of their proceeds to charity organizations (Post, 2023).

Perhaps you are good with computers. There are plenty of job sites on the internet where you can find remote work. For example, you can manage other people's social media accounts, or become a freelance writer. The best part about online work is that you do not have to commute to your job (if you're worried about not owning a car yet). All you need for your remote job is a computer or laptop, a fast internet connection, and a quiet space at home to do your job. If you're good at what you do, you'll have no problem getting recommendations and landing more work, which could further increase your income.

Maybe you are wondering if it's legal for teenagers to start working before they turn 18. According to the Fair Labor Standards Act (FLSA), 14 years is the minimum age for employment in the United States of America (United States Department of Labor, 2019). However, the number of labor hours for minors below the age of 16 is limited. The FLSA also prohibits minors to work in unsafe environments such as excavation, operating power-driven equipment, and driving. Another important thing to note is that each state has its own laws relating to employing minors. Ensure that you check the labor laws in your state before seeking employment.

THE BENEFITS OF STARTING WORK AT A YOUNG AGE

The one reason you may want to find a job is to make money. As a student, you probably rely on your monthly allowance from your parents. A part-time job could be just what you need to afford basic necessities and small treats such as going out with your friends. And while it can be difficult to juggle work and school at the same time, working at a young age does have many benefits. Besides earning money, you have an opportunity to gain work experience and improve your people skills. There's also no harm in setting aside funds toward your college tuition from a young age. It is actually a responsible thing to do to secure your future.

Making money while you are young also improves your money management skills. You learn to earn, save, and invest. These are important lessons if your goal is to build wealth long-term.

Besides making money, how else can you benefit from starting work at an early age? Getting into the job market while in school can help you develop your personal and professional skills in the following ways.

You Develop Important Skills

Working at a young age can help you develop key skills such as problem-solving, attention to detail, working well with others, and taking initiative. You learn how to work in a team setting or alone. A job comes with responsibilities; you have to manage your time wisely and learn how to handle your superiors, for example. These are all skills you can develop and carry across different roles in the future.

Be prepared to make some adjustments, because at work, things are a little different than in school. You'll meet different people with distinctive mindsets and personalities. Some people will be flexible and accepting. Others may be difficult to deal with. Through these experiences, you'll learn to deal with contrasting personalities with professionalism and emotional intelligence . Developing your interpersonal skills can also improve how effectively you communicate with others. It can teach you to accept people's differences in opinion and help you understand them better.

You Build a Network of Friends

Whether you are a social butterfly or you are shy to talk to people, a job offers you an opportunity to meet new people and expand your circle of friends. If the job does not offer the experience in the field you want to pursue, you will, however, build connections in the professional world. For example, you may meet someone who works at a firm you are looking to get an internship at. This gives you an opportunity to find out more about their internship program and how you can improve your application. So, treat each person you meet with respect, and keep in mind that some of the conversations you have could, one day, open doors for you professionally.

Besides making professional connections, working is a great way to make new friends and enhance your social life. You may even learn new ideas and about other cultures from working with different people.

You Build Your Self-Confidence

When you gain experience in your work, you can confidently say, "I can do that." This in turn helps you to further develop your skills and build confidence to take on new opportunities that present themselves.

You Build Your Resume

While in college, it can be advantageous to have a few skills and work experience before graduating to help you obtain internships. With time you will gain more experience in your field of study and can remove irrelevant roles from your resume.

Working at a job or different jobs can help you build your resume. The experience of solving work-related challenges can help you build credibility. Without first-hand experience, you cannot relate to issues faced in the work environment, such as resolving conflicts with coworkers and clients.

Every job comes with its own pressures and challenges. Learning to be flexible and easily adapt to change can help you thrive in the work environment. Before making the decision to start working while in school, you must take into consideration some of the downfalls of juggling school and work at the same time.

THE DISADVANTAGES OF WORKING AT A YOUNG AGE

While starting work when you're still in school has many benefits and can help you develop important life skills as well as give you financial freedom, it can also have an impact on your studies and your mental health. A job comes with its own pressures, and if you are not emotionally equipped to handle work challenges on top of your studies and personal life, you may end up feeling overwhelmed.

To help you make an informed decision, let's look at the disadvantages of working while in school.

Increased Stress

School is challenging on its own. There is pressure for students to excel academically. Those in high school work hard so they can get accepted into good colleges. The pressure of sending out college applications and trying to figure out the next phase of life can be overwhelming for students.

College students, on the other hand, work hard toward graduating top of their class. Adding the pressure of dealing with clients and work responsibilities can leave you with less energy for your studies.

You Have Less Free Time

If you are still in school, your focus should be on your studies and obtaining your college degree. You do not want to be dealing with work pressure while you have an important exam or project to work on. Besides school and work, you also need some time to yourself to practice self-care and to socialize with your friends.

If you can, create a balance between your job and your studies. Follow a daily routine. If you can set aside hours for work, studying, and your personal priorities, you will have a better chance of successfully managing your time and overall well-being.

Distraction From Your Studies

While having a job can help you gain financial independence, it can distract you from your studies. Spending hours at work means you sometimes get home too tired to study. This can affect your concentration in class and may lead to poor academic performance.

Cuts Your Childhood Short

Work can take up your time; time you can spend doing the things you love and that make your childhood memorable.

In adulthood, you may not remember what you did with your first paycheck, but you will have memories of all the beautiful places you visited, the people you met, the games you played with your friends and family, and how you expressed yourself through art or music. So, when making the decision to find work, ask yourself where your priorities lie right now.

WAYS TO MAKE MONEY IN YOUR TEENS

Now, here's the fun part. If you've been eagerly waiting to learn how you can make money to buy a new iPad or build up your financial portfolio, technology has opened us up to a whole new world of income-generation. Nowadays, you can work from anywhere in the world—part-time or full-time. You can easily turn your passion into a source of income. All you need is a computer, a reliable internet connection, your skill, and your time.

Let's explore some of the jobs you can do to earn you money while studying. There are plenty of jobs for students in different sectors. In this section, I have placed them in three categories.

- Holiday or summer jobs
- Internships
- Online jobs

Holiday or Summer Jobs

Holidays are an excellent time to find a job. You'll have the time to work and not have your job interfere with your studies. There are plenty of holiday jobs you can consider doing.

Babysitting

If you love spending time with kids, try babysitting. There's always someone who needs a babysitter. You do not require much to become a babysitter, but you do need to be at least 16 years old. Obtaining first aid and cardiopulmonary resuscitation (CPR) certifications are an added advantage, though. The American Red Cross and other local organizations offer training and provide recertification when your certificates expire, usually after two years.

Besides the first aid and CPR certificates, other skills you need to babysit successfully include excellent communication, a passion for helping children, and creativity. You must be able to communicate clearly and follow instructions, and you'll need your creativity and passion to come up with activities that will keep kids safely entertained while their parents are gone.

Landscaping and Lawn Mowing

Most people do not have the time to clean their yards and mow their lawns. This is a great business you can start for yourself. Of course, you'll need to be creative to land clients and grow your business. For example, you can add planting garden beds or raking leaves to your services.

If you are good at your job, you will have no trouble landing clients by referral.

Become an Event Photographer

In this age of social media, everyone wants digital copies of their memories. From birthday parties to family gatherings, if you have a good eye and a good camera, you can take photos and edit them at a fee. Typically, a flat rate is charged for a defined number of photos from the event, with the ability for the client to add additional images at a fee per image. You can also charge more for the production and delivery of physical prints.

Become a Lifeguard

This can be a great summer job and an excellent way to earn extra cash. You get to work flexible hours and the pay is good; most lifeguards get paid more than the minimum wage.

To become a lifeguard, however, you need specialized training. So, be sure to check out the requirements first and receive proper certification. If you are a good swimmer, you can consider adding swimming lessons to the services you provide and earn more.

Teach Music Lessons

Are you passionate about music? Why not teach music lessons? This is a fun way to earn money while doing something you love. Whether you play the piano, violin, or drums, you can use your experience to teach kids and adults alike how to play a musical instrument. You can have your students come over to your house for the lessons, or you can go to them.

Become a Golf Caddy

Do you live near a golf course? Get a job as a golf caddy. Your responsibility as a golf caddy would be to carry golfers' bags, hold the flagstick, clean golf balls, replace divots, and ensure the smooth running of golfing rounds. If you have a passion for golf, you will have an opportunity to learn about the game while making some money.

Dog Walking and Pet Sitting

If you own a dog and have experience with taking care of animals, consider starting a dog walking and pet-sitting business. Some people may want to travel for a short period of time and need someone to watch their pets while they are gone. This is where your services come in. You can start your business in your neighborhood and charge a fee to walk your neighbors' dogs.

If you are looking for part-time work, pet sitting is a great way to earn money during holidays. You take care of the pet for a few days while the owner is away and get paid for it.

Make and Sell Art

If you are creative and love art, start a business making jewelry pieces and sell them online on sites such as Etsy, or at art shows and craft shops. If you love painting, get your paint brushes and find inspiration to create some beautiful works of art and sell them online. If you own a camera, consider selling your photography to sites such as Shutterstock, Adobe Stock, or iStock photo. If you take pictures as a hobby, just for fun, why not monetize them? This is a great way to make money while doing what you love.

Internships

An internship is a great way to have a feel of the industry and role you would like to pursue in your career. Internships can help you gain experience, improve your skills, and gain a better understanding of the working environment when making a decision about which career path to pursue. They are also great for adding work experience to your resume.

If you're about to graduate from college and wondering how an internship can help you on your career path, here are a few benefits internships offer students.

The Benefits of Internships

Gain Work Experience

Job vacancies usually have a minimum work experience requirement. If you're looking for a job soon after graduating from college, chances are you do not have work experience—an internship offers you that. Interning in a firm or company in your field can help you gain the experience you need to land the actual role.

Build a Professional Network

Working in a professional environment is a great way to meet people in your field. Fostering professional connections and networking are important skills to cultivate in your career journey. The people you add to your network can connect you to job opportunities and recommend you to their own networks.

Build Your Research Skills

If, for example, you're in the science field, you'll have an opportunity to test the research skills you learned in school in a real lab. From this experience, you can decide what lab role you would like to pursue in the future.

Be Mentored in Your Field

Internships offer the opportunity to meet the best professionals in your field. Through networking in the organization, you increase your chances of meeting a potential mentor who will guide you on your career path in your chosen field.

Inform Your Career Goals

While studying for a college degree can help you decide what career path to pursue after graduation, an internship can help you decide the type of jobs that fit your personality and set of skills. You will also have an opportunity to receive career advice from industry professionals.

Increase Your Chances of Being Hired Permanently. Often, hiring managers offer permanent positions to eligible interns. If you have a great personality, are good at what you do, and are passionate about your work, you might just be employed permanently by the end of your internship.

Build Your Confidence

The change from being a college student to working a full-time job can be exciting and overwhelming at the same time. An internship offers you an opportunity to work in a real-life setting. The experience of putting your skills and knowledge to work can help you build the confidence to apply for your future job.

Secure Good Recommendations

The managers and supervisors you'll work with for the duration of your internship are important in helping you build credibility in your career. If you do a good job and showcase competence in interpersonal relations, you'll not have a problem being recommended for positions by managers.

Where Can You Find an Internship?

There are two types of internships: paid and unpaid. A paid internship offers an opportunity to gain experience in your field and be financially compensated in the process. An unpaid internship, on the other hand, does not pay you for the work you do financially, but it's still a great way to put your skills to use and gain valuable experience.

Where can you apply for internships? Applying for an internship can be daunting, but the good news is the internet is filled with job sites where organizations post internships that you can apply for. This does not mean ignoring the traditional route of reaching out to your social network for referrals. It simply means by searching the internet as well, you increase your chances of getting an internship by sending applications to more than one organization. The other advantage of searching the internet for internships is that you can narrow down your search and focus on the roles you have an interest in.

Let's explore some of the job sites you can use to apply for internship programs.

LinkedIn

Most human resource managers search for potential candidates on LinkedIn. This makes LinkedIn a great platform to build a professional profile that could land you an internship. All you have to do is create your profile, upload a professional picture, and detail your education, skills, and work experience. Doing this will make it easy for people in your field to find your profile.

Once your profile is complete, connect to your professional network, which should mostly be other people who are in your field, former instructors or classmates, and creators you can follow in your chosen industry. To apply for internships, use the LinkedIn search bar to search for internship programs. You can narrow down your search and search for paid and unpaid internships.

LinkedIn has an "Easy Apply" feature that allows you to send your application and resume with just a click. This saves you the time of searching for the email addresses of companies. You can also follow the organizations you have an interest in interning for to stay updated on the projects they are working on.

Google

Google remains one of the best search engines on the internet. All you need to do is search for paid or unpaid internships in your field; for example, marketing or accounting internships, and different sites related to your search will pop up.

Indeed

Indeed is another job listing platform you can use to search for part-time jobs, internships, and freelancing gigs. You can refine your search by defining job title, salary range, and location which can help you find the job you are interested in.

On Indeed, you can search for different organizations, go through their company profile, and reach out to recruiters on the chat feature. You can also upload your resume and save it on Indeed and save yourself time when applying for posts.

Glassdoor

Glassdoor is a global job search platform that allows you to search for internship openings, company reviews, and descriptions of job interviews. You can gain a better under-standing of the organization by going through its profile and reading reviews left by present and former employees.

With Glassdoor, you can easily apply for jobs or internships and select your preferred salary range from a range of pay packages from different companies.

Idealist

A non-profit organization, Idealist is an excellent job board to search for internships on. You can find listings from different organizations focused on making a social impact across the globe. Idealist even has a section for searching for internships, specifically. You can refine your search by specifying your location, the type of organization you want to work for, and the compensation plan. You can also create an email alert and get notified when there is a new job listing you may be interested in on the site.

Global Experiences

Global Experiences is an international internship website that offers internships to students and young professionals at a fee. The website offers both online and onsite internships in different places and for different programs. Global Experiences offers career readiness programs and guaranteed internships and one-on-one advisors to help you choose an internship program that best suits you and your career goals.

And there are many other job listing websites you can search for internships on.

- **Coolworks.** This site offers an opportunity to work in amazing places such as national parks, ski resorts, camps, ranches, and on the water. The site has a feature where you can search for recently posted internship opportunities.
- **InternAbroadUSA.** This is a great internship site if you are open to working in a foreign country. After completing the registration process, the site matches you with recruiters and companies that align with your internship program expectations.

InternAbroadUSA also helps you with the entire onboarding and Visa application process.

- **Mediabistro.** If you're in the media and advertising industry, you can find internship opportunities on the Mediabistro website. The site matches those pursuing a career in the media, broadcasting, advertising, and marketing with companies. Mediabistro also offers courses and webinars to empower you in your chosen field.

- **SimplyHired.** If you're looking for an entry-level job or customer service role, you are likely to find vacancies on SimplyHired. So, there's no need to worry if you're not skilled at any role yet; there are plenty of low-skill roles posted on this site.

- **Monster.** This site offers a variety of postings, from entry-level up to executive roles. It is free for job seekers and has an app you can download. Whether you're looking for a part-time or permanent job, in-person or remote work, you're likely to find vacancies on Monster.

ONLINE JOBS

If you are tech-savvy, you're at an advantage. Technology is evolving, and a lot of companies are utilizing the internet to increase their revenue. Most companies have moved away from the traditional ways of advertising, like using paper posters and fliers, to using social media marketing tools and online platforms to advertise their products and services.

If you are wondering what you can do online that can earn you some extra cash, or even help you save up for a car or for your college fund, try looking at your current skills. What are you good at? Do you have excellent writing skills, perhaps? There are plenty of companies looking for content writers to pen their social media posts, blog articles, press releases, business proposals, website content, and other advertising and marketing content.

Whether you are looking for a part-time or permanent job, or you are looking to start your own online business, there are plenty of opportunities for you to make money online. Here are some ideas you can explore to help you decide what job best suits your skills and personality.

Blogging

Setting up a blog requires a few tech skills and choosing a domain name for your blog that will be easy for people to remember when searching for your content online. Once you set up your blog, you can blog about anything that excites you; whether it's animals, fashion, sports, personal development, your life as a student, or personal finance.

Keep in mind that it may take time for your blog to start generating income, but with time, it can grow into a great business. Blogging can also improve your research and writing skills for college and life in general. To generate income, you can add affiliate marketing services and Google AdSense to your blog. Once you have set up your blog, you must regularly add articles and videos to it to keep your online audience engaged and increase your website traffic.

Freelance Writing

If you have excellent writing skills, you can turn your skills into a freelancing business. This could also be an excellent way to develop your writing skills, which will help you in your career path. If you enjoy writing, this is one way to make money while doing what you love!

Freelance writing requires you to pay attention to detail, be able to write and proofread your work, and have access to a computer with a reliable internet connection . You'll not have difficulties finding individuals and companies looking to hire writers on websites such as Fiverr, Upwork, LinkedIn, and other freelancing sites.

With freelance writing, you must pick a niche you are passionate about or knowledgeable in. It could be sports, personal finance, or business. Having a specialized niche can help you master your craft; the more you write on a particular topic, the higher your chances are of becoming an expert in it.

You can work as a ghostwriter, as well. There are companies or individuals looking for people to write their blog articles, eBooks, workbooks, and other eLearning material anonymously. Although as a ghostwriter you do not get credit for the work you do, you'll get financially compensated for your work.

Freelance writing offers plenty of opportunities to make money online. For example, if you have set up your blog, you can write your own books on topics you are passionate about and sell them on it. You can also sell your books on sites such as Amazon and start earning passive income.

Social Media Management

With businesses building their online audiences and searching for ways to reach more people, most bloggers and entrepreneurs are looking for people to manage their social media accounts on Instagram, Facebook, Twitter, TikTok, or Pinterest. If you're creative, have excellent writing and communications skills, and are up to date with social media trends, you can start a social media management agency. You can also offer to write website content for individuals and companies, manage their emails, and help businesses grow their online reach.

Social Media Content Creator

If you follow social media trends and have a specific niche you are passionate about—for example, fashion, beauty, or finance—create content on topics related to your niche. If you are passionate about makeup, why not become a makeup and beauty influencer? You'll have an opportunity to work with the brands you love and get paid for promoting their products.

To increase your revenue, you can introduce affiliate marketing and earn a commission for marketing products with a discount code for companies. So, if you have great planning and scheduling skills, why not become a social media content creator?

Graphic Designing

If you are tech-savvy, graphic designing is another lucrative business you can start. Graphic designing involves making websites for individuals and companies and creating visual concepts to communicate information. Graphic designers create posters, billboards, company logos, packaging, and other marketing material.

You can take an online course to learn how to become a graphic designer. YouTube is also a great place to find video tutorials on how to develop your design skills. As a beginner, you can start learning and practicing graphic design on Canva.

Canva is an online design site that has great design tools, and most of them are free. However, if you'd like to have the full experience and access all their design tools, you have to sign up for Canva Pro and pay a monthly subscription fee. You can use Canva to design social media posts, create flyers, posters, and presentations, as well as edit videos.

Start a YouTube Channel

YouTube is one of the most popular ways to make money online currently. You can create different content on your YouTube channel. For example, you can create funny videos of jokes, video tutorials on topics you are passionate about, and make music videos or short story films for entertainment.

It takes time to master creating and editing videos and coming up with content that people actually want to watch, but once you get the hang of it and understand your followers and their needs, a YouTube channel can turn into a good source of income. You must be 18 years and older to start a YouTube channel.

How do you generate revenue through a YouTube channel? One way you can generate income through a YouTube channel is by running advertisements. You simply earn money from the ads that appear in your videos. You can also earn through membership subscriptions and have your subscribers pay a monthly fee for exclusive content.

Become a Virtual Assistant

With a lot of businesses going digital, some companies are hiring virtual assistants to take care of all administrative tasks. As a virtual assistant, you are more like a personal assistant, but working remotely. Your duties include managing emails and social media accounts, booking appointments, scheduling meetings, coordinating with suppliers, liaising with clients, handling customer complaints, and organizing the company's data.

If you have excellent people and organizational skills, you can earn money working from the comfort of your home as a virtual assistant. Most companies post job listings for virtual assistants on sites such as LinkedIn and Indeed. Ensure that your profile is professional and up to date, and create an alert so you get notified each time a virtual assistant job listing is posted on these sites.

Play Video Games Online

Most teenagers love playing video games. Why not find ways to get paid while doing what you love? Video game developers often need people to test out their new games and give them feedback. Sites such as Inboxdollars and Mistplay offer players a chance to earn money for testing out new video games and providing their feedback. Some of these sites even have gaming contests where you can participate and win cash prizes while perfecting your gaming skills.

If you have a YouTube channel or are thinking of starting one but struggling to find a niche, why not create content and do gaming reviews?

Teach a Second Language

If you speak other languages—for example, Portuguese, French, Spanish, German, Mandarin, Japanese, or Italian— you can get paid for teaching a second language to people online. If English is the only language you speak, you can also teach English to people from foreign countries who are not native English speakers.

There are plenty of other opportunities to earn money.

- Working in retail stores as an assistant.
- Working at a grocery store as a cashier.
- Delivering groceries. You can sign up on sites such as Amazon Fresh, Fresh Direct, Shipt, or Instacart to do this. (Note that you must be at least 18 to sign up for work on delivery apps.)
- Working at a restaurant.
- Working at a movie theater.

HOW TO LAND YOUR FIRST JOB

Now that you have an idea of the type of job you want to look for, let's explore ways in which you can prepare yourself for your job search. Finding work can be a difficult process, even for people who have experience. It can be more challenging if you have never written a resume before, have been to a job interview, and do not have work experience. The good news is, you can prepare yourself beforehand for your job search to make the entire process less overwhelming.

The following ideas will help you start your job-hunting process.

Decide on the Type of Job You Want

When searching for a job, you must take a few things into consideration to help you decide on the type of job you are looking for. For example, what is your desired schedule? Do you want to work more hours within a limited time frame? Seasonal jobs and internships might work for you.

You also want to consider your current skills and interests. For example, if you have excellent people skills, enjoy working from home, have great organizational skills, and love working with people from different backgrounds and cultures, you could look for a job as a virtual assistant.

Taking into consideration the skills you want to develop and the type of environment you want to work in can also help you decide on the type of job to pursue. For example, working in retail would mean you either work as a front-of-house assistant or in the warehouse, whereas if you work as a landscaper, you'll work outdoors and often in different locations.

Search for Job Opportunities

Once you figure out the type of job that matches your skills and interests, you can now start your search on different job listing platforms. There are different channels you can use to search for jobs.

- Company websites
- Online job boards

- Shops in your area
- Newspapers

If you want to work for a specific company, your best bet would be to visit their website and check if they have any vacancies. Some companies also advertise vacancies on their social media platforms. You can use online job boards such as LinkedIn, Indeed, Glassdoor, ZipRecruiter, and many others to search for your desired job.

While it's easier to search for jobs on the internet, do not ignore traditional ways of job searching. For example, your local shops. There are places that post vacancies on their store windows. You could talk to the shop owner or supervisor and find out if they're looking to hire entry-level employees.

Get a Work Permit if You Need One

Some companies may require you to have a work permit for you to be employed. Usually, these requirements depend on the industry, your age, and your location. Be sure to check what the employment requirements are in your region.

Create a Basic Resume Online

A resume is an important document when searching for employment. It states your skills and experience for the role you are applying for. If you have not worked before:

- highlight your soft skills such as communication, problem-solving, critical thinking, and work ethic.
- include any volunteering or freelancing work you've done.
- you can add activities you are involved in such as sports, music, or dance lessons.
- include any relevant school projects you have done and school awards for academic excellence.

There are different websites you can use to create a resume. All you have to do is fill in your details on a ready-made resume template. You can use www.resume.io or www.canva.com to create a customized resume.

Network

Networking is important when you are job hunting. Talk to your employed friends and ask them for advice. Learn more about their working environments and the workplace culture. Ask your parents if they know of anyone who is hiring.

Speak to your teachers, coaches, neighbors, and family connections, and find out if they know any companies who are hiring. Networking is an excellent way to get recommendations.

Prepare for Your Job Interview

After submitting your resume, you may be shortlisted as a potential candidate. If an employer is interested in hiring you, he or she will invite you for a job interview. When you receive an invitation to a job interview, prepare yourself well. Do your research on the company you are interviewing with, and prepare to answer basic interview questions such as:

- Why do you think you are the best candidate for the job?
- Why are you interested in working for the company?
- Where do you see yourself in five years?
- What skills are you learning in school that will help you with your role?
- What is the biggest challenge you have faced recently, and how did you solve it?
- Do you have questions about the role you are applying for?

Ask a friend or family member to help you prepare for the interview. You can role-play and have your friend ask the interview questions while you answer them. This will help you gain confidence when responding to questions.

Follow Up With Prospective Employers

Following up after a job interview is important. It shows your prospective employer that you are interested in the role you applied for. Wait at least a week before sending a follow up message or making a phone call to find out the status of your application.

HOW TO SUPPORT A JOB SEEKER (FOR PARENTS)

Teenagers have their own expectations of what their first job will be like. Hunting for your first job can be exciting and overwhelming at the same time. It may not be all rosy, especially for a teenager who has no experience. Their job application may get rejected, they may not be shortlisted for an interview, and they may or may not receive feedback on why their application was rejected. These are some of the things teenagers need to prepare themselves for ahead of their job search.

As a parent, your support goes a long way in the job-hunting process. Believing in your child's abilities and sharing your experiences can help them manage their expectations. There are other factors that you must take into consideration, as well, such as where the job is located, whether it is safe for your child, and if spending time at work does not affect their school activities. These questions will help you guide your child during the job-hunting process. You should also consider doing the following.

Share Advice on Workplace Etiquette

You may have some great tips and advice to share from your own workplace experiences. Offer your child advice on how to be an excellent employee, and how building a good reputation can come in handy in their career. Let them know the importance of proper workplace conduct, such as dressing appropriately, communicating well with coworkers, completing tasks on time, and being a team player.

Help Your Child Prepare for the Interview

Answering interview questions can be scary for a teenager who has never interviewed for a job before. Preparing beforehand can help your child gain confidence when answering interview questions. You can do a mock interview and role-play. Ask them common interview questions and explain the importance of proper posture and maintaining eye contact. Remind your child to prepare a few questions for their potential employer, as well, just in case they are asked if they have any questions regarding the company or the role they are interviewing for.

Introduce Your Child to the Tools They'll Need

A solid resume and professional cover letter increase the chances of landing a job. So, take some time to go through your child's resume and see if it needs to be edited. Help them write an outstanding cover letter that will inspire the hiring manager to invite them for an interview.

Talk About Workplace Safety

While it's important to support your child's decision to start working at a young age, it is equally important to make them aware of some of the experiences they may encounter in the workplace. Talk about the effects working in a toxic environment can have on mental and physical health. Advise your child to open up if any issues arise that make them feel uncomfortable, and ensure they know that they must speak to an authority figure about their concerns.

Let Go of the Reigns

Watching your child grow and begin to make decisions on their own can be a difficult adjustment for many parents; your role somehow changes from savior to supporter. You may have the urge, from time to time, to solve your child's problems. However, that will stunt their growth. Allow your child to go through certain experiences and learn how to solve challenges by themselves. Be there to listen and offer advice only when it is needed. You may want to leave work-place negotiations for your child to handle. This will help them improve their problem-solving skills.

Also, identify your child's motivation for wanting a job. For example, do they want to save up for a car? Working toward a set goal will inspire them to stay on track and work toward achieving it.

MULTIPLE SOURCES OF INCOME: THE KEY TO FINANCIAL SECURITY

The reason why people have jobs and keep searching for ways to make more money is the need for financial security. Creating different avenues that generate revenue increases your chances of financial stability. It allows you to earn more money and prepare yourself for when one or more income streams fail. You will be in a better position than someone with only one income stream.

With this new age of technology, there are plenty of ways to earn money. As we discussed earlier in this chapter, under Ways to Make Money In Your Teens, once you identify your passion and your current skills, the next step is to find ways to monetize them.

The Benefits of Multiple Sources of Income

Creating multiple sources of income is key to financial stability. It increases financial security, can help you pay off debt, allows you to afford your lifestyle, and creates a soft cushion to land on if you are hit by a financial crisis. Following are some of the benefits of having more than just one source of income.

Greater Financial Stability

While most people believe that having a job provides financial security, what happens when you wake up and the company you are working for is shut down, or you get laid off because the company cannot afford to pay you anymore? How will you sustain yourself? This is where having multiple sources of income becomes an advantage. You will have something to fall back on in case you lose your primary source of income. This reduces the stress that comes with not being able to fulfill your financial obligations and meet your financial goals.

As inflation rises, the cost of living is rising as well, which makes having more than one source of income a necessity. Generating more income puts you ahead of the economic challenges and allows you to channel some of your income into your savings and investments.

Financial Independence

What does financial independence mean to you? Does it mean paying off your student loans? Or, does it mean being able to afford your lifestyle, travel around the world, and have enough time to spend doing the things you enjoy with your loved ones? Whatever your definition of financial freedom is, having different avenues that generate income can help you live life on your own terms.

Creating multiple sources of income gives you options. For example, you can take on a job that requires you to work flexible hours. Or, you can choose to work part-time and spend more time studying and pursuing other passions. Having revenue flowing in from different avenues prepares you for a brighter financial future.

Provides an Opportunity to Work From Home

In this age of technology, the internet has plenty of opportunities to build multiple sources of income. If you prefer to work in a less busy environment, doing online work can provide you with the freedom to work independently. Depending on the type of job you will be doing, working online allows you to set your own hours and work from anywhere. It increases your flexibility and allows you to create more avenues that will generate revenue and increase your income.

Allows to Live Your Dream Life

The real reason why people look for jobs and start businesses is so they can afford their lifestyles and live the life of their dreams. Whether you are a philanthropist and want to make a difference in your family and community, or you just want to live comfortably—without the stress that comes with financial instability—being smart enough to create and manage different sources of income can help you live your dream life.

The earlier you start building different sources of income, the higher the chances of you achieving financial independence.

Allows You to Work Less

Generating revenue from different sources allows you to eventually work less. Creating passive income through selling digital products, online courses, and investments, enables you to work fewer hours. You'll eventually be able to stop trading your time for money, and instead, spend your time doing the things you love and identifying more ways to generate revenue.

Managing More Than One Job

Working while in school requires planning and careful thought. First, determine how you intend to balance your time. Also, take into consideration if it is going to interfere with your studies and well-being. Juggling too many responsibilities and failing to create balance in your life can lead to burnout and serious health issues.

To manage more than one job and prevent getting overwhelmed by work and school, you must create a balance in your life.

Getting Organized

Utilize applications such as Microsoft Outlook and your Apple or Google Calendar. This will enable you to organize tasks, create alerts for deadlines, and keep track of your projects, prioritizing the important ones. For example, you can create a spreadsheet to organize your tasks by order of priority and start working on them one by one.

Know Your Limit

It can be exciting to start seeing revenue flow in and you may be tempted to work hard and take on more projects. But, consider how this will impact the quality of your work and other areas of your life. Never bite off more than you can chew. Understand that you have limits. Taking on more work than you can handle can result in sub-standard work, which could ruin your reputation and cost you future projects.

Knowing your limits will reduce the chances of experiencing burnout and allow you to focus your attention on the projects you can handle at a given time. This will improve your efficiency and allow you to produce high-quality results.

Create a Schedule

Creating a work schedule can save time and allows you to complete tasks on a deadline. When you manage different projects without planning ahead of time, you may find yourself with multiple tasks competing for your time and attention. You may end up working on a weekend when you had planned to spend time catching up with your friends.

Find time to create a schedule. Set aside time for your work projects, your studies, and relaxing. This way, you know what you are supposed to be working on and for how long, and still have time for yourself.

Manage Your Expectations

Managing your expectations is important when juggling more than one job. You want to keep your employer informed about your other commitments and availability to avoid getting assigned more projects than you can handle. Be realistic about the amount of work you can take on at a given time, and if you're studying, factor in the time you will spend working on your school projects as well when deciding to manage more than one job.

Limit Your Commute

If you have more than one job, try to limit the time you spend commuting. Search for jobs within the same location, and if it's a walkable distance, it's even better. You will cut down on the time you spend traveling from one job to the next and save your energy for creative purposes.

Keep Your Commitments

Working two jobs at the same time requires commitment and discipline. Once you agree to take on a task, ensure that you complete it. If you are not meeting deadlines and your projects are overlapping, take some time to evaluate if you are sticking to your schedule, and consider if you need to cut down on work.

If you are focusing on a bigger task, break it down into smaller tasks, and tackle each small task at a time. This will increase your efficiency, and with time these small tasks add up. Before you know it, you will have completed the bigger project without experiencing burnout.

Take a Break

Take care of your health and take some time to rest. Giving your body time to rest has many physical and psychological benefits. It allows your entire body to reboot itself, thereby increasing your efficiency. Get your eight hours of sleep each night, and on your day off, take some time out to rest and recuperate. Catch up with your friends and family. You will be amazed at how refreshed you'll feel afterward.

Finally, if you have two or more jobs, to avoid conflict of interest, ensure that they require different strengths. For example, if one job requires you to use a lot of mental energy, the second one can be more physical to avoid compromising the quality of your work.

While working hard is important to your success, try not to overwork yourself. Take some time to rest and recuperate. Your body will thank you for it.

While learning and developing your money management skills, it's important to adhere to the law; this includes paying your taxes. Paying taxes is not as bad as most people make it sound. If done correctly, you can actually save money through taxes. Let's dive into this in the next chapter.

3

LET'S TALK TAXES

Paying taxes is not a punishment. It is a responsibility that comes with being a productive member of society.

— CHRIS MATTHEWS

Landing your first job and receiving your first paycheck is an exciting experience and a significant first step toward financial independence. However, it comes with responsibilities that you must pay attention to. Teenagers, like adults, must pay federal and state income taxes when their income reaches a certain threshold. When you start earning an income, you'll be subject to paying taxes, so it's important that you learn how to do it right.

There are two types of income used by the Internal Revenue Service (IRS) to determine when a teenager must file a tax return: earned income and unearned income. Earned income is money you earn from working at a job, such as your salary, wages, professional fees, or tips. Unearned income, on the other hand, is income earned from investments. It includes interest, royalties, rent, capital gains, dividends, and income earned from trust funds.

Based on the standard deductions for the 2022 tax year, Americans are required to file taxes if they earn $12,950 or more . If you are a minor and earn less than $12,950, you do not have to file a federal tax return. However, if you earn

$1,150 or more in unearned income (from interest and investments), you must file a tax return. If your unearned income exceeds $2,200, it is taxed at your parents' rate. What this means is, if you are a minor and earn $12,950 from your internship, you are not required by law to file a federal tax return. But, if you earn income from stock trading or through cryptocurrency investments, you may need to file for taxes (IRS, n.d.).

TYPES OF TAXES

There are different types of taxes. They fall under the following categories.

- Income tax
- Property tax
- Goods and services tax (GST)

Taxes on Income

The federal government has a progressive income system through which high-income earners receive a higher taxation rate on revenue than low-income earners. Taxes are applied through marginal tax rates. Federal rates range from 10–37% depending on the income you earn and your filing status (Fay, 2022). State and city rates are often higher. Most systems allow taxpayers to reduce their tax bill with credits, deductions, and allowances.

Income tax includes:

- payroll taxes.
- capital gains taxes.
- estate taxes.

Payroll Taxes

The U.S. government requires employers to deduct payroll taxes from their employees' paychecks and pay them to the government. These are called Federal Insurance Contributions Act (FICA) taxes. FICA taxes fund Medicare and Social Security programs. Currently, about 1% of income earned by employees goes into Medicare, while around 6% goes into Social Security (Gorton, 2021).

Self-employed individuals must pay 15,3% of their earned income; however, half of this amount can be taken as an above-the-line business deduction on an individual's income tax return (Fay, 2022).

Capital Gains Taxes

Capital gains taxes are paid on income generated from selling an asset that has appreciated in value. For example, a home sale, stocks, or bond transactions. The rate for taxation depends on how long the asset was held. Short-term capital gains from assets less than a year from their acquisition are taxed at the owner's normal income tax rate, while long-term gains from assets acquired for more than a year are taxed at a lower rate. The logic behind this is that lower rates attract more capital investments.

Estate Taxes

Estate taxes are charged on the transfer of property when the owner dies and are only charged on estates that exceed the federal exclusion limit of $12.92 million (Gorton, 2021). They are meant to prevent the extension of tax-free wealth within a country's wealthy families. The maximum estate tax rate is 40%, and some states have their own estate tax known as inheritance tax (Fay, 2022).

Taxes on Property

Also known as the ad valorem tax, the property tax is levied on a recurring basis by the local government on personal property. For example, homeowners pay property taxes monthly or annually as part of their mortgage payments.

Property taxes fluctuate based on the state assessment of the property, its condition, and market value. They are calculated using the millage rate—an amount per $1,000 of a property's assessed value (Fay, 2022).

Other assets that may be subject to property tax include cars and boats, and in some states, business property such as factories get taxed.

Taxes on Goods and Services

Sales taxes are commonly used by states and local governments to raise funds. They are charged as a percentage of the selling price of goods and services. These rates vary from state to state and differ based on the item purchased. For example, shoes may be taxed at a different rate than a meal at a restaurant.

Other taxes imposed on goods and services include the following.

- Excise taxes imposed on the quantity of an item purchased and not the value. For example, the U.S. government charges $0.18 per gallon of gas purchased (Fay, 2022).
- User fees charged on services such as airline tickets, hotel rooms, toll roads, and financial transactions.
- Sin taxes imposed on cigarettes and alcohol.
- Luxury taxes charged on luxury goods such as jewelry and high-end cars.

INCOME TAX EXPLAINED

Although there are different types of taxes, as we discussed earlier, the type of tax people are referring to when they talk about taxes is the federal income tax. This may be because it's the government's source of funds.

The federal government imposes a progressive income tax system in which the more money you earn, the more you pay in taxes.

Types of Income Tax

- Individual income tax, also known as personal income tax, is the tax charged on wages, salaries, and other income you earn. This tax is usually levied by the state.
- Small businesses, partnerships, cooperations, and self-employed individuals pay taxes on their revenue, as well. Business owners and directors compile their business income and then deduct their capital and operating expenses; the difference is their taxable business income.
- Most U.S. states charge individual income tax. These include Nevada, Alaska, South Dakota, Tennessee, Texas, Florida, Wyoming, and Washington. However, some states like New Hampshire do not charge income tax, instead they charge State and local income tax. For example, residents are required to pay a 5% tax on dividends and interest earned.

Sources of Taxable Income

Taxable income comprises both earned and unearned (passive) income. Taxable unearned income includes government benefits such as disability and unemployment benefits, lottery payments, and strike benefits. Taxable earned income, on the other hand, includes wages salaried, tips, bonuses, interest on investments, and income earned from assets owned that have appreciated in value over time. In simple terms, taxable income is income you earn each tax year.

There are different types of income types taxpayers are liable to pay taxes on, but the most common type is employee compensation.

Types of Taxable Income

- **Employee compensation.** This is money you earn from your job, such as salaries, wages, fees, bonuses, and tips, and is reported to you through a W-2 form that you get from your employer. The W-2 form shows all deductions that apply to your taxable income, such as 401(k) contributions, Social Security, Medicare, and other deductions. If you receive fringe benefits from your employer, you must include them as part of your taxable income.
- **Business and investment income.** Income from certain types of businesses such as property rental and investment activities count as part of your taxable income and must be declared.
- **Income from Partnerships.** Partnership entities are not taxed by the IRS. But, revenue made, deductions, and losses incurred in the partnership are passed

through to the individual partners. If you are a partner, you must declare pass-throughs when filing your annual tax returns.

- **Income from S Corporations.** S corporations do not pay income tax on their earnings. Like partnerships, shareholders must report earnings, losses, and deductions on their personal tax returns.
- **Royalties.** If you own rights to intellectual property such as copyrights, trademarks, and patents, the revenue you generate is considered taxable income and must be declared. Royalties also include income earned from mineral properties, oil, and gas.
- **Digital currencies.** If you make money through cryptocurrency investments and trading, all revenue earned is considered taxable income. You must declare all income earned from the sale or exchange of investments in digital currencies such as Bitcoin.
- **Bartering.** This involves the exchange of goods and services instead of cash. For example, offering landscaping services in exchange for dental services. The value of the service rendered is considered taxable income.

TAX FILING

When filing for taxes, having a checklist in place can help you get more organized and can save you time. You will need to have the following personal information and documents in hand.

Tax Prep Checklist

- Your name as it appears on your Social Security card
- Date of birth
- Social Security number or Tax ID number
- Your bank account number and routing number to receive your refund by direct deposit

The following steps will help you prepare for the filing process.

1. Determine your filing status. As a single individual who is not married, you can file for taxes as a single filer.

2. Put together all of your documents for your sources of income. The total amount from your sources of income is known as your "gross income." You will need to fill out the following tax forms to calculate your gross income (Kagan, 2019b):

a. Form W-2 shows your earned income from your jobs such as your salaries or wages.
b. Form 1099-NEC (non-employee compensation) shows income earned from contract jobs or side gigs. The 1099-NEC form reports the income you earned from non-employers if it is more than $600.

c. Form 1099-MISC shows income earned from other sources such as rentals and prizes won.

d. Form 1099-INT is sent to you by your financial institution if you earned an interest of more than $10 during the tax year.

3. Calculate your adjusted gross income. "Adjusted gross income" is defined as your gross income minus adjustments to your income such as student loan interest, education expenses, and contributions toward your retirement account (IRS, 2018).

4. Calculate your deductions. When calculating your deductions, either itemize them or take the standard deduction. A standard deduction is a set amount you pay if you do not have itemized deductions to claim. When itemizing your deductions, the following records are required.

a. Educational expenses such as tuition, textbooks, student activity fees, equipment, and supplies.

b. Charitable donation claims, which are limited to a percentage of your adjusted gross income for the current tax year.

c. State and local taxes paid. These are recorded on the W-2 form if you are employed. If you work as an independent contractor, you must have a record of the estimated taxes you paid every four months during the tax year.

d. Unreimbursed medical expenses if they exceed 7.5% of your adjusted gross income.

e. Property and mortgage interest paid. This appears on the Mortgage Interest Statement, Form 1098, sent to you by your mortgage lender.

5. Calculate your taxable income. Your taxable income is your adjusted gross income minus all your deductions.

TAX FORMS

Under Tax Filing, we learned about the types of forms you need when preparing to file your tax return. As an income earner, it's important to understand which category you fall under. Are you an employee or an independent contractor?

The Difference Between Form W-2 And Form 1099

If you are an employee, you'll receive Form W-2, an employee wage and tax statement, from your employer. It records all your benefits, compensation, and taxes deducted by your employer during the tax year. On the other hand, if you are an independent contractor (and you pay your own employment taxes), you will receive Form 1099 from the company that hired you. Form 1099 reports all payments made to you within the tax year.

During the tax season, employers must file Form W-2 with the IRS for their employees' payroll, and companies that pay contractors must issue Form 1099-MISC to employees who are not on their payroll.

Employee vs. Independent Contractor

How do you differentiate an independent contractor from an employee? According to the IRS classification, this depends on how you work and how your employer compensates you for the services rendered.

There are three categories the IRS looks at when classifying employees (IRS, 2019).

1. **Behavioral.** The company you work for controls how you do your job.
2. **Financial.** Your employer controls the business aspect of your job, such as how you are paid and who provides your tools and supplies.
3. **Type of relationship.** The company you work for provides benefits such as a pension plan, vacation pay, and insurance, and your job is a key aspect of the business.

Examples of Employees

- Staff writers, designers, and developers who work on a schedule, both online and in an office.
- Delivery drivers working on a schedule and specific routes using company vehicles.
- Project managers working on ongoing projects.

Examples of Independent Contractors

- Freelance writers, designers, and developers who work on a project basis.
- Consultants hired to work on a project with a specified start and end date.
- Gig workers who perform flexible, temporary jobs and are paid per project as opposed to an hourly basis.

THE BENEFITS OF FILING YOUR TAX RETURN ON TIME

Filing your tax return for the first time can be overwhelming, but having all your documents in place and filing early will give you enough time to plan your payments and avoid tax identity theft.

Filing taxes on time:

- Can help you avoid paying interest and penalties.
- Prevents you from losing future refunds.
- Can help you avoid the federal tax lien issued by the IRS when you neglect or fail to pay your taxes.
- Filing your tax return on time safeguards your credit and prevents you from having liens against you which can damage your credit score.
- Makes it easy to apply for financial aid to pay your education expenses.

- Gives you a clear picture of your income.
- When applying for a loan, creditors look at your tax returns to determine your interest rate. Filing your tax return on time gives creditors the confidence that you'll pay off future debts and can help you get lower rates.
- Builds your Social Security benefit. Filing your tax return on time allows you to claim income from self-employment and ensures that it will be included when calculating your benefit.
- It is the right thing to do, and doing the right thing gives you peace of mind.

WAYS TO SAVE ON TAXES

Receiving an unexpected tax bill can be a mood killer, which is why it's important to file your tax returns on time to avoid surprises. There are several ways you can reduce your tax bill and save cash in the long run.

- **Contribute to your Health Savings Account (HSA).** If you have a high-deductible health plan, you can open a health savings account. You can use this to pay for out-of-pocket medical expenses. Contributions to your health savings account are tax-deductible, while withdrawals, on the other hand, are tax-free—if you use the money on qualifying medical expenses.

- **Tweak your paycheck withholdings.** You can change your paycheck withholdings by filing and sending out a W-4 form to your employer specifying how much tax to withhold. If you have a huge tax bill during the tax year, increase your payroll tax withholdings so you owe less taxes when you file your tax return. Conversely, if you have a significant refund at the end of each year, consider reducing your withholding amount. You can change your payroll tax withholdings at any time.

- **Channel more funds into your retirement account.** The less taxable income you have after deductions, the less tax you pay. The IRS does not tax contributions made to your 401(k). Therefore, channeling more funds into your 401(k) can help you pay less tax.

- **Save for college.** Saving money for college can reduce your tax bill. A 529 plan is a college savings plan sponsored by a state or state agency. A 529 can be used to pay for qualifying educational expenses, such as tuition, books, equipment, and other qualifying expenses. The funds in a 529 plan grow on a tax-deferred basis until you make a withdrawal. Withdrawals on a 529 plan are not subject to either state or federal taxes only if you use the money on qualifying education expenses. Some states may offer tax deductions on contributions.

- **Fund your Flexible Spending Account (FSA).** If your employer offers a flexible spending account, take advantage of it. You can use the funds to pay for your medical and dental expenses.
- **Assess Mutual Funds and stock performance.** If you own investments such as securities, seek the help of a professional to assess whether or not you can offset capital gains and reduce how much you are being taxed on your investment income.

KEY THINGS TO NOTE WHEN FILING TAXES (FOR FIRST-TIMERS)

To avoid making newbie mistakes when filing your federal income tax, keep the following ideas in mind:

- Keep track of your income. For most taxpayers, excluding contractors, self-employed, and dependents, your earned income must have been $12,950 or more, and your unearned income $1,150 and above during the tax year. Be sure to include all income earned, including any interests, investments, rentals, and income from freelance gigs. Finally, you should always verify with the IRS (Internal Revenue Service) regarding the tax thresholds for filing that apply to your circumstances.
- Keep all your records in place throughout the year. This includes your medical bills, receipts for

charitable donations, student loan interest, and freelance expenses. This will help you determine whether to itemize deductions or to choose a standard deduction.

- Choose your filing status. If you are not married, you can file for your income tax as a single filer.
- Be mindful of your deadlines. Plan ahead of your tax return and give yourself enough time to gather all your documents and seek help if you need to. The earlier you file for income tax, the sooner you will receive your refund.
- Decide how you want to file your tax return.
- **IRS online forms.** You can use the electronic forms the IRS provides and file yourself .
- **Tax preparer.** If you need help, it is advisable to seek the help of a tax expert. Ensure that you trust the person or tax firm you'll be working with because you'll give out a lot of your personal information throughout the process. The IRS has a tax preparers guide to help you choose a reliable and verified tax preparer.
- **Tax preparation software.** If you need guidance filing your tax return, you can pay a fee and use a tax provider's tax software to file your federal income tax returns.
- **Free file.** The IRS lets qualified taxpayers prepare and file federal income tax returns online using guided tax preparation software at no cost.

You do not have to pay more in taxes when there are ways you can save money, and still honor your tax obligation. Take advantage of all the tax credits and deductions you qualify for to reduce your taxable income.

Managing your finances requires you to always be on top of them. You must know how much you make, where your money is coming from, and what you spend it on. Without the proper financial tools to help you keep track of your spending, it is difficult to avoid overspending. The good news is that you can have control over your finances, and here's how you can do it.

4

MONEY FLOW AND CONTROL

Used correctly, a budget doesn't restrict you; it empowers you.

— TERE STOUFFER

D o you plan your purchases, or are you an impulse spender? Making money is one aspect of building wealth and securing your financial future. The other aspect involves tracking your spending.

You may have heard a lot of financial gurus talk about budgeting and the importance of this financial tool in money management. Some people can argue that a budget is a way of restricting them from spending money as they wish, but a budget does not, in any way, restrict anyone from spending money. Instead, it allows you to determine in advance whether or not you will have enough money to spend on the things you need. A budget allows you to live within your means and prevents you from spending money you do not have.

Before we discuss the benefits of having a budget in place, let's define what a budget is. A budget is a process of planning how you would like to spend your money in relation to your earnings. It is also known as a spending plan. When you first start out on your financial journey, creating and adhering to a budget will help you develop good money habits that are key to your financial success.

A budget keeps your spending in check and allows you to track your future savings. It can also help you set your short- and long-term financial goals.

THE IMPORTANCE OF A BUDGET

Having a budget in place can help you make more informed financial decisions. When you have a record of how much money you spend each month, you will know when you need to cut down on spending in order to meet your other financial needs, like housing and savings.

Budgeting is not a one-time process; it is an ongoing process that requires you to review your plan from time to time. As your income increases, you will need to make adjustments to your budget. For example, you may want to add more assets to your investment portfolio.

The following are some of the benefits of creating a budget.

- **Prevents you from overspending.** Overspending is a huge problem in today's society, which is why we have seen an increase in credit card debt over the years. Currently, younger Americans between the ages of 18–29 have a higher credit card delinquency rate of about 9% than anyone else (White, 2020). To avoid developing the bad financial habits, such as overspending, that keep most people trapped, create and stick to a budget. Know how much you should spend in relation to your earnings and try not to spend more than what you can afford.

- **Keeps a record of your finances.** A budget tracks all income and expenditures. Having a record of all your financial transactions is an effective way to manage your finances. It shows you where you are spending too much money and allows you to strategically cut down your expenses. For example, by reviewing your budget, you may find that you are spending more on your phone bill than you need to. Budgeting allows you to reassess your spending habits and refocuses your attention on your financial goals.

- **Allows you to set your short and long-term goals.** It is one thing to set financial goals and another to actually work toward fulfilling them. If you spend your money on every shiny object you come across, you may not save and meet your financial goals. A budget is an effective way to set your short and long-term financial goals. It can help you track whether or not you are getting closer to achieving them or not. If you are spending too much money on non-essentials, your budget will show you what expenses you need to cut down on and where you need to channel those funds, instead.

- **Helps you prepare for emergencies.** Life is unpredictable. The company you work for may decide to downsize or close due to a sudden change in market conditions, and you may wake up without your primary source of income. Or, you can fall ill and be unable to work for quite some time. These life events can throw you off course if you are not prepared financially. Having funds set aside for emergencies can help reduce the stress that comes with unexpected life events. To achieve this, you must have an emergency fund in place. An emergency fund is the money you set aside specifically for the purpose of emergencies. It should cover at least three to six months of your living expenses, and you must include it in your monthly budget. You can build your emergency fund slowly by depositing an amount you can afford either weekly or monthly.

WHAT DOES A BUDGET CONSIST OF?

To create an effective budget, you must understand its key components. Your budget must take into account your income (your investments, salary or wages, interest on savings, dividends, and other sources of income) as well as your fixed and variable expenses.

Your fixed expenses are expenses that do not change, such as insurance, rent, utilities, and student loan payments among other expenses. Variable expenses, on the other hand, are expenses that you can cut back on, such as clothing, shopping, and dining out.

HOW TO CREATE A BUDGET

The first step to creating a budget is to decide the most effective way for you to keep records of all your financial transactions. You can use a notebook and pen, a spreadsheet, a budgeting app on your phone, or online budgeting templates.

The following steps will help you create an effective budget.

- **Calculate your net income.** To create an effective budget, deduct your expenses from your net income. Your net income is what you take home after tax deductions, employee programs, health insurance, and retirement plans. Using your net income instead of your total salary prevents you from overspending, under the incorrect assumption that you have more disposable income than you actually do. If you are a freelancer, keep all records of your contracts and pay to help you calculate your income, which changes based on the amount of work you take on.
- **Track your expenses.** Once you know how much disposable income you have, you can then track what you spend it on. To effectively track your expenses, categorize them into fixed and variable expenses. Be

as precise as possible when creating a budget. If you have trouble recalling all your expenses, check your credit card and bank statements. They have detailed information on all your financial transactions.

- **Set realistic goals.** Set your short and long-term financial goals. Your short-term goals should be for at least a year and go as far into the future as three years. They may include building an emergency fund, paying credit card debt, or planning a vacation. Long-term goals often take years to reach. They include saving for retirement, student loan payments, and paying off your mortgage. Getting clear about your financial goals can inspire you to stick to your budget. For example, if you are planning your next vacation, you can easily identify areas where you can cut down your spending and channel more funds toward saving for a relaxing getaway trip.

- **Create a plan.** When you are clear about your net income, have an estimate of how much you spend each month. Include both your fixed and variable expenses in this calculation. Next, compare your total expenses to your net income and your financial goals. Try and be as realistic as possible when setting your spending limits while doing this. To help you set a realistic budget, divide your expenses into what you need to have and what you want to have. For example, the cost of commuting to work can be classified under needs, and dining out under wants. This allows you to identify where you can cut down on unnecessary spending and where best to redirect funds to in order to achieve your financial goals.

- **Adjust your spending to stay within your budget.** After recording your income and expenses, identify if there are wants you can spend less on such as dining out. Search for places that offer lower prices on goods and services, and take advantage of special deals. This will prevent you from overspending and allow you to stay within your budget. Saving a few hundred bucks can go a long way in helping you achieve your financial goals.

Remember to constantly review and adjust your budget in relation to your net income. For example, as a freelancer, your income is irregular; it changes according to the amount of work you take on each month. If you take on more projects one month and earn more than usual, you may achieve one short-term goal and start saving for the next. And, if you earn less in that month, you may need to identify where you can cut back on spending.

Reviewing your budget regularly will prevent you from spending more money than you have.

THE DIFFERENT TYPES OF BUDGETING SYSTEMS

The best budget depends on what you want to achieve. Do you want to reduce your spending, pay off debt, or build your savings? Budgeting methods are designed to help you understand and assess your relationship with money. While most of us have a similar financial goal—financial security—we also have different incomes and financial obligations. To achieve your own financial goals, choose a budgeting system that suits your needs.

Reverse Budget

The reverse budget or pay-yourself-first budgeting method allows you to put your goals and financial future first. This method is best suited for people who want to prioritize savings but find it difficult (Schwahn, n.d.).

Whether it's your education expenses, savings account, or retirement plan, when you receive your paycheck, channel funds toward your savings goal first, then, spend what is left over on your living expenses.

Advantages of a Reverse Budget

- It enables you to reach your financial goals.
- It reduces the chances of impulse buying.
- You can easily set up your budget with automatic tools.

Disadvantages of a Reverse Budget

- It may require that you adjust your lifestyle.
- It requires a lot of discipline.
- It is not suitable for people who live from paycheck to paycheck.

Zero-Based Budgeting

The zero-based budget is best suited for over spenders. It may not be suited for people with irregular incomes (Home Owner, n.d.). When using a zero-based budget, you start your budgeting from scratch and do not build on a previous budget. You evaluate your current situation—your net income and expenses—and decide where to cut down on spending.

The zero-based budget aims at getting your income to equal zero. This does not mean splurging on every shiny item you come across. It simply means every dollar you earn must have a clear spot to account for it.

Advantages of a Zero-Based Budget

- It ensures that every dollar you earn has a purpose.
- It is a simple and efficient way to budget for beginners.
- You can combine it with another budgeting method such as the percentage budget.

Disadvantages of a Zero-Based Budget

- Because you do not categorize your expenses, it makes it difficult to control your expenses.
- It makes you focus more on your expenses rather than on your financial goals.

The 30/30/30/10 Budget

A goal-based budget aims at helping you fulfill your financial goals. It involves setting four primary goals in different categories. For example:

- spending 30% of your income each month on your necessities, such as utilities, medical expenses, groceries, and transportation.
- channeling 30% of your income toward your financial goals such as your savings account, investments, and paying off debt.
- spending 30% on housing expenses, such as mortgage, property taxes, and rent.
- spending 10% on your wants, such as dining out, entertainment subscriptions, vacations, and shopping.

This budgeting method is suited for people who have financial goals that require a substantial amount of money and desire to prioritize them (Schwahn, n.d.).

Advantages of a 30/30/30/10 Budget

- It allows you to achieve your goals faster.
- It puts your expenses in categories so you can separate your needs from your wants.

Disadvantages of a 30/30/30/10 Budget

- It is not ideal for people who live from paycheck to paycheck.
- It depends on your location. Some areas may not be ideal for saving 30% on housing expenses because of high housing costs (for people who are renting or paying a mortgage.)

The 50/30/20 Budget

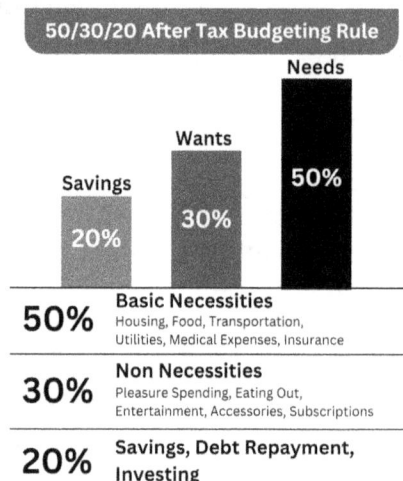

50/30/20 After Tax Budgeting Rule

Savings — 20%
Wants — 30%
Needs — 50%

50%	**Basic Necessities**	Housing, Food, Transportation, Utilities, Medical Expenses, Insurance
30%	**Non Necessities**	Pleasure Spending, Eating Out, Entertainment, Accessories, Subscriptions
20%	**Savings, Debt Repayment, Investing**	

This rule originated in a book titled All Your Worth: The Ultimate Lifetime Money Plan, written by Sen. Elizabeth Warren and Amelia Warren Tyagi.

This budgeting method splits your income into three categories: 50% allocated to your needs, 30% toward your wants, and 20% toward your savings and debt payment.

Advantages of a 50/30/20 Budget

- It allows you to track where your money goes each month.
- You can save money and still have some cash left over for your hobbies and fun stuff.

Disadvantages of a 50/30/20 Budget

- It may not be ideal for people who earn less income.
- It allocates more funds toward wants than toward savings.

The 60/40 Budgeting Method

The 60/40 budget focuses mainly on helping you achieve your short- and long-term goals (Schwahn, n.d.). When using this budgeting method, you channel 60% of your income toward your needs and 40% toward your goals.

- **Needs.** You will spend 60% of your income on rent/mortgage, groceries, medical expenses, transportation, and paying off debt.
- **Financial goals.** You will split the remaining 40% between four different financial goals.

- 10% allocated to your short-term goals, such as vacations, building an emergency fund, or paying off small debt.
- 10% to your long-term goals, such as purchasing a property, buying a car, student loan payments, and all your financial goals that may take years to fulfill.
- 10% to your retirement savings.
- 10% allocated toward wants such as entertainment subscriptions, shopping, dates, and recreational activities.

Advantages of a 60/40 Budget

- It focuses more on your financial goals.
- You can easily cut back on unnecessary expenses.

Disadvantages of a 60/40 Budget

- It may not be ideal for beginners and those with a few financial goals.

The Debt Avalanche Method

This budgeting method allows you to pay off your debts, starting with the ones with the highest interest rate (Shiundu, 2022). The debt avalanche method is best suited for people with more than one debt and a desire to clear their debt fast and cost-effectively. The aim of the debt avalanche method is to clear expensive debt first; however, if you can, channel a minimum payable amount toward small debt to avoid defaulting.

Advantages of the Debt Avalanche Method

- By paying off debt with higher interest first, you save on the interest you would otherwise pay if you keep the debt for a longer period.
- It can help you pay off your debt fast.

Disadvantages of the Debt Avalanche Method

- It is not suitable for people with irregular incomes. You need to have money coming into your account each month to cover your payments and still be able to pay for your living expenses and savings.
- It may not be suitable for people who earn less income.

The Debt Snowball Budget

The debt snowfall budget is similar to the debt avalanche method, but it focuses on paying small debts with a lower interest rate first (Shiundu, 2022). Paying off smaller amounts first and seeing your debt balance reduced inspires you to keep eliminating your debts one by one.

Advantages of the Debt Snowball Budget

- You can channel more funds to pay off your bigger debt after eliminating the smaller ones.
- It allows you to tackle the easier task first so that you are not overwhelmed by the process of paying off debt.

Disadvantages of a Debt Snowball Budget

- You may end up paying more in interest over time.

HOW TO STICK TO YOUR BUDGET

Creating a budget is quite easy. Once you have a clear picture of your net income, you can start allocating funds to different categories and account for every dollar you earn. But adhering to your budget is a whole different ball game altogether that requires discipline, and it can prove to be difficult for most people. For instance, if you are a freelancer, you can spend months without landing gigs and you end up with less income to channel toward your financial goals. The good news is that there are strategies you can use to help you stay on track.

Below are a few ideas that will help you stick to your budget.

- **Never spend more money than you have.**
  Budgeting can prevent you from overspending. If

you want to purchase a pricey item, try saving for it instead of reaching for your credit card. If you want to travel overseas on holiday, plan for it. Having a savings plan in place prevents you from deviating from your budget.

- **Stick to a lower credit card limit.** Credit cards with a higher limit can be attractive, but they may keep you trapped in debt. While using a credit card is helpful in building your credit score, using it recklessly can result in increased debt. The temptation is not worth it. It will only delay you from achieving your financial goals. Stick to a lower credit card limit and pay it off regularly to avoid defaulting.

- **Sleep on large purchases.** Before committing to making a large purchase, first ask yourself if you need the item. If you do, take some time to think about it. Do your research and find out if you can get a better deal on it. Also, take into consideration if the item you want to purchase will add value to your life and not throw you off budget. Take your time before committing to making a big purchase; you may find that you do not need it, after all.

- **Pay yourself first.** When you receive your pay, learn to pay yourself first. An effective way to do this is to automatically transfer funds from your bank account into your savings account. Choose an amount that you can afford based on your budgeting plan, and remember, the amount does not matter. Small amounts add up with time. Developing the habit of paying yourself first reinforces a savings-oriented mentality. When you start seeing your savings grow you'll be inspired to stick to your plan.

- **Connect your spending to your work.** When you understand the number of hours you put in at your job to earn money, your perception of money will change. For example, if your hourly rate is $7.25, and you work 40 hours per week, when you want to purchase a $200 item, divide the amount by your hourly rate to arrive at the number of hours you need to put in to afford the purchase. Approaching your budgeting in this way will reframe your mindset and change your relationship with money.

- **Plan your meals.** This will help you avoid buying food you do not need that will end up going bad. Further, planning your meals beforehand can help you build healthy eating habits. You buy only the things you need for your meal plan. So, choose your favorite recipes and enjoy the process of budgeting while staying healthy.

- **Take a no-spend challenge.** Also known as a spending freeze, a no-spend challenge can help you keep your spending habits in check. You can do the challenge for a week, a month, or an entire year if you like. Identify only your necessities and only spend money on those. Set how long you will take on the challenge, and invite your friends and family members to make the experience more fun.

Other ways that can help you stick to your budget include the following.

- **Cut down on subscriptions.** How much do you spend on entertainment subscriptions each month? If you are not sure, look at your bank statement. All those $10 subscriptions add up with time. That is money you could channel toward your savings account.
- **Shop for groceries online**. Purchasing groceries online can prevent you from making spur-of-the-moment purchases and overspending.
- **Compare brands before making a purchase.** Some brands are more expensive than others, but basically have the same function. Before purchasing a pricier brand, ask yourself if the quality of the item is worth the extra money you are paying for it.

While saving and sticking to your budget is extremely important to your financial well-being, do not forget to celebrate small wins from time to time. You do not want to end up grumpy and lose the motivation to save because you are on a budget. Budget for a vacation, or treat yourself to a small gift after reaching one of your goals, for example, after paying off a small debt. This will motivate you to stick to your budget and keep you on track toward achieving your financial goals.

CREATING A SINKING FUND

We have explored different types of budgeting systems and their pros and cons. Not every system will work for you. Therefore, it's important to pick a system that resonates with your current circumstances. Perhaps you have chosen to be a freelancer and you are getting a lot of freelance gigs—you now need a new laptop with a higher speed so you can keep up with all the work. But, you are worried that your monthly income cannot cover your savings, debts, living expenses, and a laptop all at once. What would be the best solution for your problem? A sinking fund!

While it's important to build an emergency fund, you also need a sinking fund to help you save for bigger purchases.

A sinking fund allows you to set aside funds each month toward specific expenses. For example, a new laptop. To effectively create a sinking fund, you must categorize it to enable you to allocate funds to each category every month. A sinking fund is best suited for expenses such as the following.

- **Medical expenses.** Health care is quite expensive nowadays. An emergency doctor's appointment can be costly and stressful if you are not financially prepared. Even with your health care insurance, still set aside funds to pay for out-of-pocket health expenses.

- **Vacation.** Planning to take a break and explore a different city or country in the summer? A sinking fund can help you save up for your dream without worrying about money.
- **New braces.** Not everyone needs braces, but, if you do, saving up for them will be a wise decision, because they are quite pricey.
- **Christmas.** Prepare for holiday expenses beforehand through a sinking fund to avoid overspending.
- **Clothing.** Create a sinking fund for your seasonal clothing such as winter coats and boots. Setting aside money for your clothing expenses also comes in handy when you have to attend a work event or wedding. You simply use your savings to purchase an outfit without the stress of going off budget.
- **Gifts.** Save for birthdays, anniversaries, Mother's Day or Father's Day, and other holiday celebrations. You do not have to save a large amount for this category, which makes it easier to save.
- **Home furnishings.** Are you planning on buying a new bed? A sinking fund is a great way to save money for home furnishings. Instead of asking yourself where the money will come from, set aside funds every month for the next six months. Not only will it allow you to stick to your budget, but it

will also help you to meet your goal of buying a new bed.

- **Tuition.** You can include your education expenses in your sinking fund by taking up a 529 college saving plan. You can use the tax advantage account to pay for qualifying education expenses such as books, tuition, and equipment.
- **Charity.** Giving back to the community, whether it is your local church or non-profit organization, can help those in need; it also gives you a sense of purpose. Setting aside funds for charity work allows you to give without holding back. If you have not found an organization to give back to, a charity sinking fund ensures that you have money saved up when you finally find a cause you believe in.
- **Yearly Subscriptions.** If you pay yearly subscriptions for things like software, prepare for them in advance. Create a sinking fund for all your recurring expenses to avoid unexpected costs and stay within your budget.

How to Create a Sinking Fund

Now that you are familiar with what a sinking fund is and how it works, here are the steps to help you set up your sinking fund and start saving for your expenses.

- First decide what you want to save, for example, if you want to save for a holiday vacation in December, allocate an amount you can afford to do without each month to your sinking fund.

- Set a Timeline. Knowing how long it will take to achieve your goal will help you calculate how much you need to save each month to reach your goal. For example, if you want to save $1,500 toward your vacation and start saving at the beginning of the year, you will need to save $136,36 each month for 11 months.

- Decide Where You'll Keep Your Sinking Fund. There are budgeting tools such as PocketGuard that you can use to automate the process of allocating funds to your sinking fund. All you have to do is link the budgeting tool to your bank account and it will set aside the amount you want to save in your budget. This way you can track how much you have in your sinking fund. If you decide to open a separate savings account, be sure to check the bank charges and that the account does not have a minimum balance. You do not want to save each month only to discover that part of your savings went into bank charges.

- Include Your Sinking Fund in Your Budget. Whether you use a spreadsheet or a notebook and pen to create your budget, ensure that your sinking fund is included to avoid skipping even a single contribution.

EMERGENCY FUND VS. SINKING FUND

People often think an emergency fund is the same thing as a sinking fund, but they are different. Before we go further in understanding their differences, let's first define what an emergency fund is and why you need one.

Suddenly falling ill and becoming unable to work can impact your finances. Without your monthly income, it will be difficult to pay for your living expenses and still save and stick to a budget. This is where an emergency fund comes in handy. As described in Chapter 4, an emergency fund is money you save each month for emergency purposes. Life is full of surprises, and an unexpected life event can leave you feeling overwhelmed if you are not financially prepared.

The Purpose of an Emergency Fund

The main purpose of an emergency fund is to save money for unexpected expenses. Here are a few other reasons why you need to build an emergency fund.

- **You stay far away from your family.** If you live in a different city or country, traveling home for emergencies can be costly. A last-minute flight ticket is more expensive than when you book your flight early. Having money saved can reduce the stress that comes with unexpected expenses.
- **You are a homeowner.** If you own the house you live in, you may need to repair your plumbing

system. An emergency fund can save you from the stress of waking up with a burst water pipe and having to pay a plumber to have it fixed with money you don't have set aside.

- **Health issues.** Falling ill can be costly and can leave you unable to work and earn an income. If you are an independent contractor, the inability to perform work activities can significantly impact your finances because you rely solely on the projects you take on to earn money. An emergency fund can help you get through those tough times when you are unable to work.

- **You are an independent contractor.** Working as an independent contractor means you work on a contract basis. Once the project you are working on is completed and your contract expires, you will not be getting paid anymore. An emergency fund can help you pay for your living expenses while searching for new projects.

- **If you are new to budgeting.** If you are just starting out on your financial journey, you may not be aware of all your expenses and accidentally leave some out of your budget. An emergency fund will help you pay for any unexpected expenses that you did not plan for.

- **You have one source of income.** Having a single stream of income puts you at a disadvantage in this era we live in where the cost of living is skyrocketing. If you lose your primary source of income you will not be able to pay for your living expenses or maintain your lifestyle. Having at least six months of living expenses saved up can ease stress if you were to lose your job.

- **You want to minimize debt.** Having an emergency fund can prevent you from accumulating more debt. When you have funds saved up you can easily pay for your car repairs or out-of-pocket health expenses that you may have left out of your budget. Using funds from your emergency fund will prevent you from taking another loan to pay for unexpected expenses and keep you on the path to achieving financial freedom.

Places to Keep Your Emergency Fund

It may be a good idea to open a savings account with a higher interest rate that is easily accessible in case of an emergency. You do not want to deal with bank issues and be unable to access your funds when faced with a crisis.

Your emergency fund account must be separate from the account you use for your daily expenses to avoid the temptation of spending your savings. Open a savings account with a bank or credit union that insures funds with the Federal Deposit Insurance Corp. (FDIC) or the National Credit Union Administration (NCUA) to ensure that your funds are protected. The FDIC and NCUA protect your money in case your FDIC OR NCUA bank fails.

Online-only banks are a better option for building an emergency fund. They charge lower fees and offer higher yields. High bank charges can chip away at your savings, which is why it's important to compare savings account rates and features.

Prepaid cards are another option. They are separate from your bank or credit union. You can load funds onto them, and you are restricted to spending only the amount on your card.

Keeping your funds in cash at home is an option, but it is riskier because cash can get stolen and you may be tempted to spend it. You also do not earn any interest on this money.

How to Build an Emergency Fund

Now that you understand what an emergency fund is, as well as its purpose, let's get into detail on how you can set one up for yourself.

- **Have a target.** Having a goal in mind can help you stay motivated to save. An emergency fund can be that goal, and will help you stick to your savings plan.
- **Set the amount you want to save.** Decide on how much you are going to save each month.

- **Have a piggy bank.** A good old piggy bank comes in handy if you are saving for your emergency fund in cash, and for smaller amounts of money.
- **Automatically move money into your savings account.** If you decide to open a savings account, automate recurring transfers to your emergency fund. Decide if you will transfer funds every week or monthly. Try and keep the amount the same, but, if you increase it, will benefit you in the long run.
- **Assess and adjust contributions.** Monitor your progress from time to time. You can either check your bank balance or write down each amount you save in a notebook. Adjust your contributions if you need to. If you have extra cash to spare, contribute a bit more than you usually do. Your saved up funds will come in handy in the future.
- **Save your tax refund.** You receive your tax refund once a year, and saving it can significantly boost your emergency fund. When you file your tax return, use your emergency fund account for the direct deposit to avoid the temptation of spending it on other expenses.

The Difference Between a Sinking Fund and an Emergency Fund

As we discussed above, a sinking fund is for specific expenses such as a getaway trip or buying a new piece of furniture. An emergency fund, on the other hand, is for unplanned expenses such as out-of-pocket medical bills or paying for your living expenses if you lose your primary source of income.

Sinking Fund

- Is for planned expenses; a specific goal.
- How long you save funds for depends on the amount of the item or goal you are saving for.

Emergency Fund

- Is for unexpected expenses.
- The ideal timeline is to save enough to cover three to six months of living expenses.
- It does not have a single purpose. The aim is to have something to fall back on when the unexpected suddenly hits you.

CASH FLOW

When you begin your personal finance journey, you must understand where all your money comes from and where it goes. This is known as your "cash flow." Money management requires you to have a thorough understanding of your cash flow.

Cash flow is your income minus your expenses over a specific period of time. You can measure your cash flow each month to see how much you make and spend.

Your income can include:

- your salary or wages;
- interest from your savings account;
- capital gains from selling stocks and bonds;
- and, dividends from your investments.

Your expenses may include:

- school books and supplies;
- tuition;
- entertainment subscriptions;
- rent;
- utilities; and,
- transportation.

The Importance of Managing Your Cash Flow

Understanding your cash flow is vital for the success of your financial future. It can give you insight into where you spend your money and where you need to cut down on spending. You can then channel the reallocated funds toward your savings. Awareness of how much you earn and spend each month can help you create a budget and stick to it. This enables you to live below your means and avoid debt, which can deter you from achieving your goals and keep your cash flow negative.

Managing your finances requires that you make smart decisions. If you want to be financially independent or purchase your dream house in the future, you want to ensure that you stay cash flow positive.

How to Manage Your Cash Flow

To manage your cash flow, you must create a budget and track all of your expenses. Below are three ways to do this that will help you stay on top of your financial goals.

- **Automate your savings.** Prioritize paying yourself first by sending funds to your savings account immediately when you get paid. This will prevent you from spending money on other expenses and improve your cash flow.
- **Use the 50/30/20 budgeting system.** When you get paid, allocate 50% of your income toward your living expenses, 30% toward your wants, and 20% toward your savings.
- **Cut back on your expenses.** Understanding your cash flow can help you identify where you need to cut back on spending. Start with your monthly expenses. For example, you may want to cut back on some of your entertainment subscriptions.

SETTING UP A BILL DUE DATE CALENDAR

A surprise bill can mess up your entire month if you are not financially prepared for it. To effectively manage your finances you must always be one step ahead. Save for emergencies before they occur and plan for all your bills before your payment due dates to avoid stress.

If you struggle to keep track of all of your bills, try creating a bill due date calendar. This will help you track all of your bills and their due dates, and helps you to better prepare yourself financially for any unexpected costs or losses.

To create a bill due date calendar:

1. Put together all your monthly bills.
2. Next, write down what the bill is for, how much you owe, and the due date. You can use a notebook or spreadsheet for this purpose.
3. Place the calendar where you will see it every week to ensure that you do not forget to pay your bills.

One other important thing to remember is that if you are making in-person or automatic payments, set a reminder on your smartphone one or two days before your due date to avoid making late payments and possibly incurring fees.

BUDGETING SOFTWARE

Budgeting software is useful in money management and can help you develop good money habits. The budgeting app you choose to use will depend on your experience with money. Whichever app you choose, the objective is still the same, and that is to help you budget effectively, save and invest your money, and spend responsibly.

Here are some budgeting apps you can explore as a beginner.

• **Mint** is a free budgeting app that can help you manage your credit cards, checking accounts, and investments. The app also allows you to create a budget and makes it easier to track your spending.

• **Tip Yourself** is a habit-building app that can help you save and develop good money management habits. Pay yourself each time you do something good. For example, when you stick to your monthly budget, or if you plan an exercise routine and actually manage to go for a run; tip yourself, even if it's just $5. These small amounts add up with time. Your money will be transferred from your checking account to an FDICinsured NBKC bank (HuffPost, 2019).

• **Plan'it Prom** is an excellent app for planning for prom night. The Plan'it Prom app can help you plan and budget for your prom without the stress of breaking your bank account. The app has a prom countdown feature, timeline, and budget calculator that makes it easy and fun to plan for your prom night.

• **FamZoo** works well if you receive an allowance from your parents. They offer prepaid cards. Your parents' card serves as the funding source for the allowance transferred to your prepaid card. Your parents retain full control of your profile dashboard on the website, but you can log in separately to monitor your spending. FamZoo also allows you to create a budget, savings plan, automated "I Owe You" (IOU) tracking, and bill payment (FamZoo, n.d.)

• **BusyKid** offers most of the features you need to start managing your finances. It allows you to earn money, budget, save, and invest. This platform also offers a prepaid card which you can use anywhere where Visa cards are accepted. Your parents can transfer your allowance from their card to yours. The bonus feature, really, is that the BusyKid app allows teens to invest in the stock market and watch it grow over time. The app not only allows you to monitor your spending, but allows you to set your savings and investment goals, as well. To avoid skipping contributions, consider automating your savings.

The app is free, but, if you use their prepaid Visa card, BusyKid charges a $4 monthly subscription fee.

• **Greenlight** offers a debit card you can use that has full parental control. You can check your balance before going to splurge to see how much you have in your account and prevent being embarrassed when you overspend and your card is declined. The app also allows you to save money and earn interest (from your bank) on your savings.

BUDGET WORKSHEET

Creating a budget worksheet is an excellent way to keep track of your spending. Using the sample below, create your own budget worksheet that resonates with your current situation, your expenses, and your financial goals.

Monthly Budget

Monthly Income

Income	Amount
Salary	
Allowance	
Gifts	
Chores	

Monthly Expenses

Fixed Expenses	Cost
Savings	
Transportation	
Tuition	
School supplies	
Utilities	
Groceries	

Flexible Expenses	Cost
Phone bill	
Gym membership	
Streaming services	
Dates	
Gaming apps	
Gifts	
Shopping	

Charity	Amount
Donations	

Other	Amount

Financial Goals

Short-Term Goals (six months up to a year)

Take driving lessons
Save money for a new laptop

Mid-Term Goals (one year up to five years)

Save funds in my 529 college plan account
Buy a used car that is worth $10,000
Save funds for my vacation

Long-Term Goals (five years and above)

Purchase a new vehicle
Save for a down payment on a house

We have learned so much about how you can gain control of your finances. Most wealthy people understand the importance of saving and investing to build wealth. They also monitor their spending by having a budget in place. They understand the importance of knowing where every dollar they earn goes, and they set clear goals for their future.

In other words, financial success requires you to have a financial road map that will help you navigate your way through both the good and bad financial times. You must learn to control your spending and avoid impulse purchases. Plan for all your purchases, and you will be well on your way to achieving your financial goals.

Spreading Financial Wisdom

Knowledge is like money: To be of value it must circulate, and in circulating it can increase in quantity and, hopefully, in value.

— LOUIS L'AMOUR

We started our journey by looking at the millionaire mindset for a reason.

Whether your goal was to make sure you have a firm grasp of all things money before you reach the adult world, or you have your eye set on making big money *now*, you're driven. You were determined to take the bull by the horns and learn everything you could about personal finance because you knew how much of a difference it would make to you going forward... and if you weren't driven before we started talking about the millionaire mindset, I'm sure you are now!

There's an excitement in getting into that mindset, and it's an excitement that can also be found in helping more people whip their personal finance knowledge into shape. Now you've got the bug for it, why not take the opportunity to spread it?

The good news is, that's dead easy to do... All it takes is a few minutes and a handful of short sentences.

By leaving a review of this book on Amazon, you'll show other young people where they can find everything they need to know to understand not just how money works, but how to make it work for them.

Because financial literacy isn't something that's taught in schools, there are so many young people out there looking for this guidance, and now that you've found it, you're exactly the right person to help them.

Thank you so much for your support. It might not seem like much, but it's going to make a big difference to someone else.

Scan the QR code to leave a review!

5

BE A SMART SPENDER

Never spend your money before you have it.

— THOMAS JEFFERSON

Imagine for a second that you had enough money and could afford the life you desired. What car would you drive? Where would you live? What places would you visit and what would you do for fun? Most people dream of living a better life, but, only a few wake up each day and live their dream life. The select few that have discovered the secret to building wealth no longer dream about that life, they live the life they have envisioned for themselves. They understand the laws of money and know how to make them work in their favor.

Money is attracted to people who know how to multiply it. When you find ways to increase your earnings, money flows to you. But how do you resist the temptation to spend money on the things you want? The truth is, it takes time and practice to develop good money habits, and the results are fruitful and long-lasting.

Taking responsibility for your finances can keep you out of debt and help you maintain a good credit score, which increases your chances of getting approved for a credit card or loan.

If you want to manage your finances, watch your spending habits. Are you an impulse buyer, or do you plan for all your purchases? An awareness of your spending habits can help you devise strategies to prevent you from splurging.

BREAKING BAD SPENDING HABITS

There are many reasons why people overspend. It may be that they are not aware of their spending habits, or they estimate their income and expenses incorrectly, and in the end, they spend more than they earn. To avoid making the same financial mistakes, here are a few bad spending habits you want to watch out for and avoid.

• **Paying for convenience.** Technology has made life easy for us. You can order food and it will be delivered to you in the comfort of your home. If you need to go out on a date, you simply request an Uber, and the Uber driver will drop you off at your destination. All this happens with just a click of a button; the payment is made online, and you no longer have to worry about carrying cash. You can pay for anything you want—if you can afford it.

While paying for convenience saves you time, you end up paying more for goods and services. For example, paying for an Uber ride will cost you more than walking to the subway, and ordering takeout is more expensive than cooking at home. So, before taking out your bank card to make that online purchase, stop and consider the cost.

- **Spending Without Budgeting.** Managing your finances requires you to be one step ahead all the time. If you are an impulse buyer and do not plan your purchases, saving and investing will feel like climbing a mountain. So, create and stick to a budget, ensure that you spend less than you earn, and you will avoid going broke and maxing out your credit card.

- **Impulse Buying.** Often, people impulse buy items such as clothes and food. When making the purchase, it may seem like it costs a small amount, but these tiny expenses add up over time, and you will soon realize that you spent a significant amount of money that could have gone into your savings.

- **Spending without tracking your expenses.** Not keeping a record of your expenses and scheduled payments can have disastrous results on your finances. In Chapter 4, we discussed different budgeting apps you can use to keep track of your spending. Pick one that resonates with you or simply use the budgeting worksheet you created at the end of that chapter.

- **Retail Therapy.** How often do you go to 7-Eleven to buy comfort food? Not only are these trips bad for your health, but they are bad for your budget, as well. Spending money because you want to make yourself feel better is not a good reason to dig into your savings; and, it will probably just end up making you feel worse in the long run. Whether it is buying a chocolate bar or a new pair of jeans, stop and reflect on your financial goals before making the purchase.

How to Break Bad Spending Habits

A positive mindset toward finances and a few good decisions can set you up for a successful financial future. Now that you are aware of your detrimental spending habits, let's look at some ways to develop healthy spending habits.

Wait Before You Spend Money

Setting financial goals means that they are important to you and you want to achieve them. Achieving anything of great magnitude often takes great sacrifice and discipline.

When you hold off making certain purchases, you allow yourself to focus on your goals, for example, paying off college tuition—and before you know it that debt that once looked like a mountain will be reduced to zero and you can focus on other goals.

Understand Your Motivations

We all have strengths and weaknesses. An awareness of your tendencies can prevent you from sabotaging your financial future. Remember, at any given moment, you can make a choice that will bring you closer to your dream life or drive you further away.

Stick to Your Budget

Creating a budget is the best way to monitor your spending. Without an itemized list of your income and expenses, it will be difficult for you to track your spending.

A budget allows you to allocate every dollar you make into different categories so that you can account for it. Stick to your budget, and you will avoid overspending and making impulse purchases.

Reduce Credit Card Spending

Credit cards are very useful. They can be used for emergencies. When paid on time, a credit card can help build your credit score. However, credit cards should not be used for purchases that you cannot afford.

NON-NEGOTIABLE VS. DISCRETIONARY SPENDING

There are two types of spending: non-negotiable (meaning things you need to buy), and discretionary (the things you want to buy). When you create your budget, categorize your expenses into needs (expenses you cannot live without) and wants (expenses you desire but don't need).

Examples of Needs

- Rent or mortgage
- Utilities

- Health care and therapy
- Food
- Work uniform
- Transportation

Examples of Wants

- Entertainment
- Monthly subscriptions
- Streaming and internet services
- Home purchases
- Electronics
- Travel
- New clothing
- Dining out

The Difference Between a Need and a Want

Needs	Wants
A need is an essential requirement that must be fulfilled in order for you to survive.	Wants are desires or luxuries that add comfort to your life but are not essential to your survival.
Needs are limited.	Wants are unlimited.
Needs do not change with time.	Wants change as your desires and interests change.
When needs are not fulfilled they can negatively impact your well-being.	Wants are not essential and will not have much of an impact if left unfulfilled.

PAYMENT METHODS

There are many different ways to make payments when making purchases, and each has its advantages and disadvantages. When choosing a payment method, always prioritize safety and ensure that the payment method is secure.

Cash

Most small businesses, such as retail shops and coffee shops, accept cash payments.

Advantages of Using Cash

- Using cash to make purchases eliminates transaction costs.
- Paying cash makes budgeting easier.
- Cash payments prevent overspending.

Disadvantages of Using Cash

- ATM withdrawals come with a fee.
- Cash can be stolen.
- Unless you have the time to put together all the receipts for your purchases, paying cash for goods and services can make it difficult to track your spending.
- Paying cash does not build your credit score because you are not using credit.

Checks

When a check is deposited, it is cleared through the bank. Money is removed from the check writer's account and deposited into the check receiver's account.

Advantages of Using Checks

- Checks provide security because they must be signed by the recipient who must provide their identity document prior to cashing the check.
- Excluding potential costs for printing and mailing, checks usually have lower fees.

Disadvantages of Using Checks

- Ordering a checkbook can be costly depending upon the type of checks ordered and the delivery method used.
- It takes longer for the bank to process a check— usually one to three business days.
- Checks are susceptible to fraud and they can bounce if you have insufficient funds in your bank account.
- Nowadays, many places do not accept checks.

Debit Cards

Debit cards are directly connected to your bank account. A debit card can be used both to remove money from an ATM and to make purchases.

Advantages of Using a Debit Card

- With a debit card, you can withdraw cash from an ATM.
- You can purchase goods and services directly at shops without using cash.
- Prevents overspending because you can only spend the money you have in your account.
- You won't get charged interest because payments are made directly from funds in your account.

Disadvantages of Using a Debit Card

- Debit cards limit your spending to your account balance.
- Financial institutions charge fees on overdrafts.
- Making payments using a debit card does not build your credit score since you are not using credit.

Credit Cards

Credit cards are similar to debit cards but differ in functionality. Credit card companies such as Visa, Mastercard, American Express, and Discover offer credit to buyers and cover the purchase price. As the borrower, you pay the credit card company every month. In other words, rather than paying the seller directly, you pay off the bill to the credit card company. If the entire balance of the bill is not paid, the credit card company will charge interest on the remaining balance. You can use a credit card to make online purchases and at physical retailers.

Advantages of Using a Credit Card

- Credit cards can help you build your credit score, which comes in handy when you want to acquire a loan or make larger purchases.
- You can earn rewards and airline miles when you use a credit card and save money while traveling.
- They pose little risk of loss as opposed to carrying cash.

Disadvantages of Using a Credit Card

- If used irresponsibly, a credit card can result in debt.
- Credit card companies charge high interest rates on unpaid balances.
- Defaulting on paying your credit card balance can negatively impact your credit score and make it difficult for you to acquire a loan when you need it.
- You can incur processing fees from merchants, making the cost of purchases higher than other payment methods.

Mobile Payments

Nowadays, most point of sale (POS) terminals have a contactless payment option that can read your banking information through an app installed on your smartphone. Contactless technology requires you to set up a mobile wallet with your card information. Once your phone reads the information on the POS system, and payment is processed, you will receive a notification about your purchase.

Advantages of Using Mobile Payments

- Mobile payments are fast—a tap with your smartphone and authentication is all that is needed to complete payments.
- You only need your phone to process transactions.
- Mobile payments provide security through tokenized mobile payment apps.
- They also provide extra security through biometric authentication requirements on your mobile device.

Disadvantages of Using Mobile Payments

- Mobile payments are still new, therefore they are not widely accepted.
- If you lose your mobile phone or your battery dies you will not be able to make payments.
- Contactless technology is only supported by certain types of mobile phones.
- You may be required to use a specific app when making purchases, for example, Apple stores only accept Apple Pay.

Electronic Bank Transfers

Wire transfers are often used for making large or frequent purchases. Employers also often use electronic transfers to pay their employees. Bank transfers send money from your bank account to the seller's account.

Advantages of Using an Electronic Bank Transfer

- Electronic payments are faster than other payment methods.
- They are perfect for paying recurring expenses such as subscriptions and loan payments.
- Your payment history has all your transactions and can be helpful in tracking fraudulent transactions.

Disadvantages of Using an Electronic Bank Transfer

- The downside to using an electronic bank transfer is that you must have the funds in your account.
- You may pay higher transaction fees.
- And, funds may not be recoverable for certain types of electronic bank transfers.

CREDIT CARDS VS. DEBIT CARDS

Choosing the best payment method depends on your needs. Before choosing to use a credit card or a debit card, be aware of the pros and cons of both payment methods.

Credit Cards for Teens

Using a credit card from a younger age can teach you how to use credit responsibly. If you are below the age of 18, you can become an authorized user of your parent's credit cards. When you turn 18, you can then apply for a credit card of your own.

The best credit cards typically have low credit requirements and low costs. Here are a few options you can choose from based on your needs.

Deserve® EDU Mastercard

If you want a credit card with low credit requirements, Deserve® EDU Mastercard is the best option. There is no security deposit required and you do not need your parents to cosign to acquire their credit card.

Other advantages of the Deserve® EDU Mastercard include:

- A one-year membership on Amazon Prime when you spend $500 on your first three billing cycles (Credit Karma, n.d.)
- You receive $1 cash back on all purchases.
- Deserve® EDU Mastercard does not have an annual fee.

Petal® 2 Visa® Credit Card

Petal® 2 Visa® card does not charge fees on late payments, foreign transactions, or an annual fee. Other benefits of using the cards are:

- There's no security deposit or credit history required to acquire the credit card.
- It has a money management tool to help you keep track of your spending and manage your finances.
- It offers rewards. You receive 1% cash back on all of your purchases, and up to 1.5% on qualifying purchases after making 12 on-time monthly payments (Brennan, 2017).

Capital One Platinum Secured Credit Card

The Capital One Platinum Secured card gives you an initial limit of $200 and requires a $49 deposit. If you would like a higher credit limit, a higher deposit will be required.

If you want to build your credit fast, the Capital One Platinum Secured card is a better option. Your credit activity is sent to the three credit bureaus, Equifax, Experian, and TransUnion, and you could be considered for higher credit in less than six months (Brennan, 2017).

The downside of using the Capital One Platinum Secured card is that it does not offer rewards, but you still get reasonable deposit requirements and no annual fees.

Debit Cards for Teens

Debit cards can be a safer way to spend money. Using a debit card can help you learn how to control your spending because you can only spend what's in your account. It is safer than carrying cash around and you have a record of your expenses, which can help you create a budget.

Take caution when using a debit card because they're also prone to the risk of fraud. If you are under 18 your parents can set up parental control so they can monitor any suspicious activity and limit data-sharing companies from accessing your sensitive information.

When choosing the best debit card, just like when deciding on which credit card to use, you must understand the advantages and disadvantages of using each card.

Here are a few options you can choose from.

Greenlight Debit Card

Greenlight is one of the most popular budgeting tools for kids that offers a debit card. Your parents can send your allowance from their bank account directly to your card and you can use your card anywhere Visa cards are accepted.

Greenlight has three plans you can choose from: Greenlight Max, Greenlight Core, and Greenlight Infinity (Zimmer, 2023). The plans differ in pricing.

Advantages of Using the Greenlight Debit Card

- Greenlight allows you to earn compound interest from your bank on growing balances.
- It is user-friendly, even for a beginner.
- Your parents can set up chores for you and automatically pay you when you complete a task.
- You can create a budget on the Greenlight app and allocate funds toward your savings, expenses, and investments.

Disadvantages of Using the Greenlight Debit Card

- Greenlight charges a monthly fee of $4.99 to $14.98 (Lake, n.d.).
- They do not accept money transfer apps such as Apple Pay, Venmo, or PayPal.
- They do not allow cash deposits.
- The basic plan offers limited benefits.

The BusyKid Debit Card

This is an affordable debit card if you are learning to grow your savings. BusyKid allows you to save and invest money in the stock market.

Advantages of Using the BusyKid Debit Card

- BusyKid does not charge fees for loading money or inactivity.
- There is no age restriction to acquire the BusyKid Debit Card.
- Can be used to make contactless payments, such as Apple Pay.
- You receive your account balance notifications to avoid declined purchases.

Disadvantages of Using the BusyKid Debits Card

- Charges $1.50 per ATM withdrawal.
- It may take a while to load money on the card if you do not make automatic deposits.
- Charges a fee for card replacements.

GoHenry Debit Card

GoHenry offers a personalized debit card, allowing your parents to set up chores for you and pay you for every completed task. You can use this debit card to make contactless payments, and they have 45 card designs to choose from.

Advantages of Using the GoHenry Debit Card

- Makes it easy for you to receive your allowance and gifts from your family and friends.

- You receive real-time transaction notifications, which makes it easy to track your spending.
- GoHenry accounts are FDIC-insured (GoHenry, n.d.-b).
- You can easily block and unblock your card.
- The GoHenry app has a secure PIN recovery feature.
- Blocks unsafe spending categories such as alcohol and gambling.

Disadvantages of Using the GoHenry Debit Card

- Does not offer FSCS protection (Lauren, 2023).
- You do not earn interest on savings.
- You have to call or email the support team to close your account.

IS BUYING IN BULK WORTH IT?

With the high cost of living, finding ways to save and cut down on expenses is a smart thing to do. One of the many ways you can do this is by buying household essentials in bulk. While it may seem like you are spending more money at the time of making your purchases, buying essentials you use on a daily basis in bulk saves you money in the long run. And, if you buy from a wholesale supplier, you are most likely to get the unit price of each item at a lower price than when buying a single item from a grocery store. So, next time you decide to go grocery shopping, remember, it is cheaper to buy certain goods in bulk than as single items.

Besides saving you money, bulk buying:

- **Reduces waste.** When you buy in bulk you reduce the need for excess packaging, which is good for the environment and you have less weekly household waste.
- **It is cost-effective.** Buying goods in bulk from a wholesaler is cheaper than buying from a grocery store. You only pay for the product you are purchasing and not for the extra packaging.
- **It saves transport costs.** Buying in bulk means you make fewer trips to the store. This prevents you from impulse buying and the cost of transporting the goods.
- **It encourages conscious shopping.** By creating a list of the things you need, you avoid buying things you do not need. In other words, bulk buying encourages mindful spending.
- **It is more environmentally friendly.** Bulk purchases have less packaging than small purchases. Plastic packaging is a threat to the environment and a huge problem in today's world. Finding sustainable ways to manage waste can help save our planet.

Products to Buy in Bulk

- Cleaning and laundry supplies
- Toiletries
- Rice
- Canned goods
- Dried beans

Products to Avoid Buying in Bulk

- Eggs
- Fresh fruits and vegetables
- Milk
- Meat (if you buy meat in bulk ensure that you freeze it)
- Bread and bakery produce
- Baking products
- Spices

MANAGING SUBSCRIPTIONS

Almost everything these days has a subscription fee. Streaming services, software, gym memberships, and internet plans all take a portion of your income. If you are not mindful, you may end up racking up unnecessary subscription fees.

With new, exhilarating shows streaming every day on entertainment platforms, it can be tempting to subscribe to both

Netflix and Amazon Prime Video. But, why subscribe to two streaming services that offer the same things? Rather, cancel the one you do not utilize the most and opt instead to save money spent on a service you hardly use.

Since almost everything has a subscription fee, you may want to find ways to effectively manage the subscriptions you need to avoid paying more in fees. To help you save money on subscriptions, here are a few ways to cut back spending on digital products.

Take Advantage of Free Trials

Before subscribing to a service or digital product, try out the free trial. This way, you give yourself time to test the digital product before committing long-term. For example, streaming services such as Amazon Prime Video give you a free 30-day trial (Code Cutters News, n.d.). This allows you to binge on your favorite shows for a couple of weeks without paying a single dollar. How cool is that?

Be mindful when subscribing to the free trial that at the end of it you will be charged for the service. Set a reminder on your phone to cancel the subscription before the trial ends if you end up deciding that you do not need or want the service.

Cancel Subscriptions With a Similar Purpose

While it may seem like you need some of the digital products you are subscribed to, when you take stock of all of them you may find certain products that have similar purposes. Identify those, and cancel them. Only pay for the products you use most. For example, if you use more than one note-taking app, such as Evernote or Notion, identify which one you use the most and cancel the one you use less.

Take Advantage of Family Plans

Some services allow password sharing, which makes it easy to share a plan with family and friends. Netflix, for example, offers a premium plan that allows up to four users to watch television shows at the same time (Loic, 2022). Why not utilize these plans and save money?

Bundle Your Subscriptions

Some companies add complementary products and services that enhance your existing subscription. For example, Spotify has an add-on subscription to Hulu, which has high-demand television shows. This makes Hulu the perfect complementary product for Spotify's subscribers who enjoy streaming music. So, instead of subscribing to different products, get a bundle subscription and save some cash.

Use a Credit Card With High Cash Back Rates to Pay for Subscriptions

Some credit card companies offer cash-back rates on services such as streaming. For example, Citi Custom Cash gives you 5% cash back on qualifying purchases—and streaming services are also eligible (Haegele, 2023). This means that the more you stream, the more money you earn.

Other ways to help you save on subscriptions include:

- Comparing plans and picking the cheaper one. You really do not have to pay more for subscriptions. Before committing long-term to a product, shop around for one that has lower fees.
- Pay for yearly subscriptions instead of choosing monthly subscriptions. Most companies give discounts to subscribers who are willing to commit to a yearly plan.

THE DIDEROT EFFECT

The world we live in today is fascinating. Most people complain that there is not enough money. It is quite understandable to feel this way because of the high cost of living. However, it is mind-boggling to observe in today's world how much money people spend on things they do not need. It makes you wonder, what are the core motivations that lead people to purchase more stuff than they need? Societal pressure is one of them. We have allowed the media to influence the decisions we make, including how we spend money. Of course, there are other factors, as well, such as internal motivations. It does not matter what your motivations are, what matters is having an awareness of why you spend money on things you do not need.

What Is The Diderot Effect?

The Diderot Effect is a social phenomenon that explains the motivations behind overconsumption that is based on the findings of French Philosopher, Denis Diderot, who lived most of his life poor back in the eighteenth century. When his daughter was set to get married, Diderot could not even afford a dowry. Despite his lack of financial success, the philosopher's name was well-known because he was the writer and co-founder of the encyclopedia at the time. The encyclopedia was literary and philosophical reference work that covered political, social, and intellectual repercussions in France before the Revolution.

Having heard of Diderot's financial troubles, Catherine the Great, Russia's Empress, offered to buy Diderot's library for £1,000, which is more than $150,000 today.

Now that Diderot had money, he decided to buy himself a beautiful scarlet robe. But, when he bought the robe, Diderot suddenly realized that the rest of his belongings were out of place, and he felt the urge to buy things that matched the robe. In short, one purchase led Diderot to another (Clear, 2015).

The Diderot Effect is based on two ideas:

1. You buy goods that complement each other and align with who you are.

2. Acquiring a new possession often creates a spiral of consumption leading to more purchases.

For example, when you buy a new shirt, you suddenly have the need to buy a new pair of jeans to go with the shirt. If the jeans fit perfectly with the shirt, you think to yourself, why not get a new pair of shoes to compliment my new outfit? Buying clothes for yourself is not bad, but the compulsive need to buy more items is a habit you want to break.

Why Does The Diderot Effect Happen?

James Clear explained this phenomenon well when he said:

Life has a natural tendency to become filled with more. We are rarely looking to downgrade, to simplify, to eliminate, to reduce. Our natural inclination is always to accumulate, to add, to upgrade, and to build upon (Clear, 2015).

It is natural that as you advance in life you want more things that align with your current self-image.

How to Avoid The Diderot Effect

Habits can be changed. At any given time you can make the decision to change your spending habits before they turn into addictions. If you are a compulsive spender, the good news is that there are ways you can begin to transform your mindset and avoid The Diderot Effect.

- **Let go of wanting things.** There will always be a new brand of car, a new iPhone, the latest pair of kicks, and so on. You must resist the urge to want things. It takes discipline to achieve this, but the results are beneficial to your financial future.
- **When you buy something new, give something away.** When you purchase a new item, give away the one you were using. This way you prevent stacking up items.
- **Purchase only what you need.** Try and resist the urge to buy stuff just to impress people. Only buy what is useful to you.
- **Set a limit for yourself.** This is an excellent way to avoid overspending on items you do not need. Set a specific limit on how much you will spend on certain items and stick to it.

Remember, you are not defined by your possessions. Your self-worth is not tied to what you have or do not have as most marketing would lead you to believe.

GET DISCOUNTED PRICES

Most people in the U.S. are not used to bargaining on price. We need to learn that retail shops offer discount codes on certain items, and if you just ask a store assistant or the manager, you may end up paying less than the price on the tag.

If you want to save money on discounted prices, here's how you can do it.

• **Sign-up for email alerts**. Most companies send discount coupons to their subscribed members. Some stores, such as West Elm, offer a discount when you sign up for their mailing list. Some of the coupons can only be used once, but, if you are smart about it and use different emails, you can get multiple coupon codes to use on your next purchase.

Remember not to focus on only one store. Check out their competitors as well to see what they are offering, and compare their prices. Next, create a folder for promotions in your inbox. This way you have all coupon codes sent in one folder, making it easier to compare prices.

• **Follow your favorite stores on social media.** Connect with your favorite retailers on Twitter, Facebook, and Instagram. Some retailers do giveaways or offer early access to a sale as part of their marketing campaign.

• **Do not fall into the dynamic pricing trap.** Most online retailers price their goods based on demand. They use the information they gather from your browsing history to understand your spending patterns and use that information to set your price point.

To avoid being charged higher prices, always delete your browser's cookies and log out of your account. You can also use the incognito window to prevent cookies from being saved each time you browse the internet.

- **Abandon your cart.** Try picking a few of your favorite items and leave them in your cart for a day or two—if you do not urgently need them. You may receive a coupon from the store to lure you to make the purchase. Stores such as Home Depot, Levi's, and many others use this strategy, and it often works.

- **Check to see if you can get a price-drop refund.** Some stores offer a price-drop refund to customers. If, for instance, you bought an item and a day later the price of the item went down. You can ask for a price-drop refund if you contact the store within a certain number of days. If you order items on Amazon, ensure that you reach out to the company within seven from the date of delivery (Lee, 2014).

- **Contact customer service: sometimes, they extend expired coupons.** If perhaps, when you receive a coupon you do not want to purchase anything and the coupon expires, contact customer service. Often, companies are willing to extend expired coupons because they want you to buy. This is not always a guarantee, but sometimes it works in certain stores.

You can also search for coupons on sites such as couponcraze.com if you are not receiving them. And, if you are using multiple coupon codes, be strategic about it. If a company offers you multiple coupons, for example, one for a 20% discount and the other for a $10 discount. Use the 20% offer first to earn a bigger discount.

At the beginning of this chapter, I asked that you take a moment to think about what life would be like for you if you had enough money. Where would you live? What kind of car would you drive? A Porsche, maybe. Whatever your dream life looks like, it is possible to achieve if you follow the rules of money and delay instant gratification. Get rid of the need to want to spend money on things you do not need. If you can, negotiate lower prices and save instead of hemorrhaging money. Avoid falling for social trends and you will save yourself from The Diderot Effect.

So far, we have learned the importance of budgeting and keeping your expenses at a minimum. We spoke about how saving money can help you channel some of it toward your student loans and other debt. While debt can damage your credit score, if not managed, it can be useful in the future when you want to make bigger purchases such as a home or car.

Next, we'll learn how you can take advantage of loans and use credit to maximize your finances.

6

THE CREDIT GAME—KNOWING THE RULES

Your credit score is the doorway to financial opportunities.

— SUZE ORMAN

I s credit all that bad? You may have heard financial gurus preach about living below your means and getting rid of your credit cards if you want to be financially free. While it is true that credit cards can land you into serious debt if not used responsibly, they come in handy during emergencies.

Debt isn't necessarily bad. It all depends on what you use borrowed funds for, which is why acquiring adequate financial knowledge is important. Good credit history builds a good credit score. Without a credit history, you put yourself at a disadvantage with creditors when you finally need to apply for a loan.

Your credit score shows creditors that you are credit-worthy and puts you at an advantage to acquire loans at lower interest rates, qualify for more credit cards, and pay lower insurance premiums.

UNDERSTANDING LOANS

A loan is the sum of money a creditor lends to a borrower for future repayment. Usually, the creditor charges interest on the principal value and the borrower must pay back both the interest and the principal balance within a certain period.

While it's advisable to save money when planning to make a large purchase, it's not always that easy. With expenses such as your college education, car, or home, you may need to borrow money to cover them. If you cannot save for a large purchase, taking out a loan would be the best option.

Loans can be one-time amounts or an open-ended line of credit available with a specific limit. In simpler terms, when you need to borrow money, you apply for a loan from a financial institution. The creditor or financial institution will then advance the sum of money you require. In return, you must agree to their terms and conditions, including the interest rate, finance charges, and repayment date among other conditions. In certain instances, the creditor may require collateral for security purposes and as reassurance of payment.

There are different types of loans out there, and knowing which one will be best suited for your purchase is vital in your decision-making.

Types of Loans

A Secured Loan

A secured loan is backed by collateral, for example, a car, or a house. The collateral is the asset for which the loan is acquired; meaning, the collateral for a mortgage is the house.

Unsecured Loan

Signature loans and credit cards are classified as unsecured loans. They are not secured by collateral. Unsecured loans typically have higher interest rates than secured loans because of the high risk of default.

Personal Loan

This type of loan covers almost anything, from emergencies, medical expenses, vacations, home renovations, electronics, and so on. Personal loans are easy to apply for. You can do it online through your financial institution, credit union, or online lender.

Student Loans

Student loans are used to pay for tuition and educational expenses at accredited schools. There are two types of student loans: federal and private. To apply for a federal loan, you must fill out the Federal Application For Student Aid (FAFSA). Inquire with your school's financial aid department for more details regarding the application process.

Federal loans have more benefits and security than private loans, but have higher interest rates. Conversely, private loans have fewer benefits, but, if your credit score is good, you may be charged lower rates.

Revolving Credit

Revolving credit is a type of loan issued by a creditor which allows the borrower to withdraw funds, repay, and withdraw again. For example, a credit card is classified as an unsecured revolving loan. Another example is a home equity line of credit (HELOC).

Installment Loan

An installment loan is generally any loan that is repaid in scheduled payments. The creditor advances the borrower with a principal amount that is to be repaid in installments. Each payment or installment includes part of the interest on the principal amount.

Fixed and Variable Interest Rate Loans

Before taking out a loan—whether you are applying for a new mortgage, personal loan, or credit card—understand the difference between fixed interest and variable interest. This will help you decide which loan is best suited for your situation.

Fixed-interest-rate loans have a fixed rate over the duration of the loan term despite changes in market interest rates. This means repayments remain the same over the payment period.

Variable-interest-rate loans, on the other hand, have flexible rates. Their interest rate changes as the market interest rates change, resulting in varying payment amounts. As market interest rates rise, variable interest rates rise. When they fall, the interest on your loan goes down, as well. Variable interest rates can be applied to mortgages, personal loans, and credit cards.

Payday Loan

This is a short-term loan that lasts up to your next paycheck. Payday loans do not require good credit. In case you cannot repay the loan in that month, payday loans allow you to roll over your loan to the following month. While this may seem helpful, the finance fees charged are high and often leave people in debt. I do not recommend ever getting a payday loan.

Auto Loan

If you want to purchase a vehicle, an auto loan is your go-to loan. Auto loans have three to seven-year repayment terms. The vehicle itself is the collateral. If you fail to pay the creditor, your car will be repossessed.

You can acquire auto loans from banks, credit unions, car dealerships, or online lenders. Most car dealerships can help you acquire a loan through their finance department. Some give you a loan which is often more expensive than acquiring it from financial institutions, so be sure to shop around before committing.

Debt Consolidation Loan

A debt consolidation loan is a loan you take out to pay your existing debt. Combining all your existing loans into one large loan may result in better repayment terms, such as lower monthly payments or interest rates.

Home Equity Loan

Also known as a second mortgage, a home equity loan allows homeowners to take up a loan against their home equity. Home equity is the part of a home that an individual owns and not the bank. The loan amount is calculated based on the current market price of the house and the mortgage balance that is due. Home equity loans typically have fixed interest rates and can be paid for up to 30 years (VanSomeren, 2021a).

Mortgage Loan

Mortgage loans are used to purchase a home. There are different types of mortgage loans available to different groups of people. For example:

- the U.S. Department of Agriculture (USDA) loan for rural and low-income earners;
- the Federal Housing Administration (FHA) loan—for low-income earners and people with a low credit score; and,
- the Veteran Administration (VA) loan for veterans, service members, and their spouses.

Banks and credit unions usually give out mortgage loans but can sell their loans to federally-sponsored entities such as Freddie Mac and Fannie May (VanSomeren, 2021a).

LOAN TERMS: COMPONENTS

Loan terms refer to the length of time it will take for a loan to be paid back if the borrower makes regular payments. The loan contract issued to a borrower by the creditor describes the rights and responsibilities of each party and the conditions for the loan.

When applying for a loan, be aware of:

- The duration of the loan.
- How much you are required to pay monthly .
- The due date.
- The financial fees involved.
- The annual percentage rate (APR).
- The interest rate, and whether it will change as market interest rates change.

Reading through the fine print and understanding loan terms is extremely important when taking out a loan. Loan terms give you an overview of what you should expect when you take out a loan. They outline all of the fees and penalties you'll incur for late payments and the grace period you'll be given before the creditor charges you a late fee.

INTEREST RATES 101

Interest rate refers to the amount charged by a creditor for lending their money. It is expressed as a percentage of the borrowed amount. Interest rates vary depending on the asset and the financial institution you acquire credit from.

Interest rates also apply to bank deposits. Banks borrow money from their clients when they make deposits and use it to give out loans. The interest you earn on your savings account or a certificate of deposit (CD) is what the bank pays you for using your funds.

How Interest Rates Work

Interest rates apply to most borrowing and lending transactions. The borrowed amount is either paid back in full as a lump sum or in monthly installments. When taking out a loan, the interest rate is applied to the loan amount. This means the amount you pay back will be more than what you borrowed. In other words, interest rates compensate the creditor for the use of their funds.

When paying monthly installments, include the interest on the loan repayment to prevent your outstanding debt from increasing. Banks typically charge higher interest rates if they perceive the risk of default. For this reason, they usually charge higher interest rates on revolving loans such as credit cards.

People with a low credit score are also considered a risk by banks and are usually charged high-interest rates in case they fail to pay back the loan. A higher credit score attracts lower interest rates.

Types of Interest Rates

Simple Interest Rates

Also known as regular interest rates, a simple interest rate is an amount due on a loan calculated based on the principal amount. For example, if you take out a $10,000 loan from a bank at a 5% annual interest rate, you would be required to pay $500 annual interest.

Accrued Interest

Accrued interest refers to the accumulated interest on a loan that has not been paid from a specific date. Accrued interest can either be interest earned by a lender or an expense incurred by the borrower. For example, if your monthly interest is $40, the loan accrual is $1,29 per day (with payment being required after a 31-day period).

Compound Interest

Compound interest, also known as interest on interest, is interest charged on the borrowed amount and the accumulated interest in the previous period. Compound interest is usually higher than simple interest and also applies to your savings account. For example, if you deposit $5,000 into a savings account that earns 5% interest annually, your annual interest earned would be $275. If you keep the $5,275 in your bank account for another year, you'll have $5,538.75 by the end of the second year. This is because you were earning interest on the increased total of $5,275 in the second year.

HOW INTEREST RATES ARE DETERMINED

The interest charged by the bank is determined by factors including the state of the economy. For example, the Federal Reserve in the U.S. sets the interest rate which banks use to determine the annual percentage rate (APR) they offer to their clients (Banton, 2023a).

If the central bank sets the interest rate high, the cost of borrowing increases. When the cost of borrowing rises, it discourages people from borrowing. Another important thing to note is that as inflation rises, interest rates rise, too. In a high-inflation economy, people often prefer to save their money because of the high interest they earn in their savings accounts.

To fight inflation, banks set higher reserve requirements, which result in a tight money supply and low demand for credit. While this is meant to cool down inflation, it affects businesses that end up with limited access to capital funding through debt. At the same time, the stock market suffers immensely in a high-inflation economy, because investors would rather save their money and earn high interest than invest in the stock market with lower returns.

When interest rates are low, borrowers have access to loans at lower rates. Since the interest they earn on their savings is low, people would rather spend their money than keep it in their savings accounts. Investors start to invest in high-risk investment vehicles such as stocks. As people begin to spend money, capital is injected into the markets, the economy is fueled, and economic growth ensues.

Governments usually prefer lower interest rates, but lower interest rates lead to an imbalance in supply and demand, which leads to inflation, and in turn an increase in interest rates.

CREDIT SCORE: THE MAGIC NUMBER

Previously, we discussed debt and the importance of a good credit score when applying for a loan. Your credit score is a crucial part of measuring your ability to repay debt. You can get your credit score calculation from the three credit bureaus in the U.S.; TransUnion, Equifax, and Experian.

Often, people are surprised when they receive different credit scores. This is not uncommon, because credit scores vary based on the company providing the score and the data and method used to calculate the score. Credit unions and other institutions such as Fico and VantageScore use different credit methods.

The type of credit score creditors use depends on the industry and asset involved. For example, when purchasing a car, car dealerships and banks use a credit score that focuses on your payment history together with other data provided by the three credit bureaus.

How a Credit Score is Calculated

Credit bureaus typically use the following factors to determine your credit score.

• **Your payment history,** Creditors need reassurance that you'll pay back the loan, which is why they look at how you've paid debt such as credit cards, student loans, auto loans, personal loans, home equity loans or mortgages, and other types of loans in the past.

Your payment history also provides insight into your late and defaulted payments, repossessions, and bankruptcies.

• **The number of accounts in your name.** A credit score also takes into account all the debt you have, including credit cards, mortgages, home equity loans, student loans, personal loans, and auto loans. Creditors look at how many accounts you have for each credit. This reassures them that you can manage multiple accounts of different kinds of debt.

• **The length of our credit history.** Credit bureaus may consider how long your oldest to recent credit account has been active for when calculating your credit score. Creditors want reassurance that you have responsibly managed your debt in the past.

• **The credit you've used compared to your available credit.** Before granting you credit, creditors want to see your credit limit. They want proof that you use credit responsibly and make regular repayments. If some of your credit accounts have exceeded the limit, this will negatively impact your credit score.

• **New credit.** New credit accounts may also affect your credit history, therefore credit bureaus may consider them when calculating your credit score.

HOW TO IMPROVE YOUR CREDIT SCORE

I hope that by now you have a clear understanding of how you can use debt to your advantage. Used responsibly and for the right purposes, debt can help you build your credit score. If used irresponsibly, it can be detrimental to your financial health. Establishing good credit habits such as making regular repayments can help you build a good credit score.

Fortunately, there are ways you can manage your credit and ensure that you maintain a good credit score.

Reviewing Your Credit Reports

Get copies of your credit report from the three credit bureaus and review them to see if there are any errors. It can also help you to identify if there have been any fraudulent transactions in your name and allow you to take any necessary action.

Make Regular Repayments

Most creditors use the Fair Isaac Corporation (FICO) scores to make lending decisions. They consider your payment history to determine whether you are creditworthy or not. In fact, your payment history makes up 35% of your FICO score (Lake, 2022). It is therefore important to pay off your debt. Start by making regular payments. To pay off debt fast and avoid paying more in interest, whenever you can, pay a bit more than what you owe. Be consistent and ensure that your payments are on time. Automating your repayments and paying them before the due date can prevent late payment fees.

Limit Your Credit Utilization to 30% or Less

Credit utilization is the amount of credit you use at a given time and is the second-most important factor (after your payment history) for determining your FICO score. To limit your credit utilization, try and pay off your credit in full each month. And, if you cannot, then limit your credit utilization to 30% or less. Ten percent is considered ideal to raise a credit score, so aim at eventually bringing your limit down to less than 10%.

Limit New Credit Requests

When applying for credit, there are two types of inquiries into your payment history carried out : a soft inquiry and a hard inquiry. A soft inquiry refers to checks done by your financial institution and credit card companies to decide whether you are creditworthy or not. This type of inquiry does not affect your credit score. Conversely, hard inquiries involve checking your mortgage, auto loans, and applications for new credit, such as for a new credit card. A lot of hard inquiries in a short space of time can ruin your credit score. Financial institutions interpret it as you taking credit because you are in financial trouble, and therefore consider you a risk.

Fatten a Thin Credit File

A thin credit file means you do not have enough credit to generate a credit score. The good news is that you can boost a thin credit file and build a good credit score. One way you can improve your credit file is by using the Experian Boost.

The Experian Boost is a system that collects all of the data that is usually excluded from your credit reports such as utility payments and banking history, and includes it in your Experian FICO score (Lake, 2022). This is a free tool designed for people with a low credit score but who have a good history of paying bills on time.

Another system you can use is UltraFICO, which uses your banking history to generate a FICO score. Ensure that you maintain your bank account over time, avoid bank over-drafts, and pay your bills on time through your bank in order to receive a good credit score.

Keep Your Old Accounts Open and Pay Off Outstanding Balances

Your credit score calculation includes how long your oldest account has been active. The older the credit account, the more creditors consider you worthy of taking more credit. Consider keeping old credit accounts open. Closing them while you have outstanding balances lowers your available credit and can negatively affect your score. So, ensure that you settle all outstanding balances and resolve all collection accounts to avoid losing points on your credit score. If you cannot make full payment on collection accounts, speak to your creditors and offer them settlements.

Consider Debt-Consolidation

Paying off more than one debt can be overwhelming. To ease the pressure on you, consider taking out a debt-consolidation loan to pay off all your debt from a credit union or your bank. Making a single payment each month is better than paying multiple debts, and if you get a lower interest rate you may be able to pay off your debt faster.

Use Credit Monitoring

Credit monitoring services such as Experian IdentityWorks^{SM} or Identity Guard are excellent for checking if there are any changes in your credit score, for example when you open a new account or pay off a balance that is due. They give you access to your credit report from one of the three credit bureaus and can prevent identity theft and fraudulent transactions. If there are inconsistencies in your credit report and accounts you are not familiar with, contact your credit provider and report suspected fraud.

Why Is Your Credit Score Important?

At the beginning of this chapter, I touched briefly on the importance of maintaining a good credit score. A good FICO score ranges between 670 and 739 (Capital One, 2021). If you use a different credit-scoring company, check their ideal scores. For example, for VantageScore, a good credit score is between 661 to 780.

A good credit score enables you to:

- Save money on home insurance. Insurance companies may check your credit history on things such as on-time payments and how much you owe to decide how much premiums to charge you.
- Get better car insurance rates. Some insurance companies use your credit score to determine what rates to charge you. They can check your credit history to decide whether to raise your premiums or not allow you to renew your policy.
- Get a higher credit limit. A good credit score makes you desirable to creditors and puts you at an advantage of getting approved for bigger loans.
- Qualify for lower credit card interest rates. A good credit score makes you eligible for a lower annual percentage rate (APR).
- Get more housing options. With a good credit score, you can get a mortgage for a home at a lower rate. A good credit score also comes in handy when applying for an apartment to rent. Some landlords consider your credit history to decide whether to approve your application.
- Apply for a cell phone contract without putting down a security deposit. Cell phone companies often require an up-front payment when you have a poor

credit score. With a good credit score, you can avoid paying up front fees.

- Get utility services quickly. Utility companies also look at your credit history to see if you'll be able to make payments. If you have a poor credit score, you may be charged a security deposit.
- Look better to potential employers. When applying for a job, some employees may look at your credit as part of your background check. Having bad credit is a red flag that could cost you a job opportunity.

GOOD DEBT VS. BAD DEBT

Up till now, we have discussed how debt can help you build a good credit score and how you can use borrowed funds to your advantage. We also touched on how using debt irresponsibly can ruin your credit score and put you at a disadvantage with creditors. Now, let's differentiate between good debt and bad debt.

First, let me say this: Despite the type of debt you incur, debt is debt. How you use it determines whether it is good debt or bad debt.

Good Debt

This is low-interest debt that can help you increase your income or net worth.

- **Student loans.** Federal student loans are an investment in your education and typically have lower interest rates. Investing in your education and obtaining a college degree could potentially open doors for employment opportunities in the future.
- **A mortgage.** A mortgage gives you a chance to be a homeowner. Taking out a mortgage can help you buy a house you can afford.
- **A home equity loan.** Borrowers take out home equity loans at lower interest rates for different reasons. You can use the loan for home improvements and increase the value of your home.
- **A small business loan.** If you want to start a business your best bet is to take out a small business loan. Starting a small business is risky. Most small businesses often fail within their first two years (Debt.org, n.d.). But, if you do your research about the industry you are venturing into, starting a small business can turn out to be a good investment.

Bad Debt

This is debt with high interest rates and the potential to derail you from achieving your financial goals.

- **Auto loans.** A car is an everyday essential which makes it easy to be mobile, but the value of most cars depreciates with time. This is why it's considered bad debt.
- **Payday loans.** While taking out a payday loan to sort out an emergency may seem like the right thing to do at the time, payday loans have a high interest rate and can keep you stuck in debt for quite some time.
- **Credit cards.** While credit cards can help you build good credit, they often have high interest rates. Credit card companies lure clients to use their credit cards by offering them rewards. This will lead you to spend money you do not have, and if you do not regularly pay your credit card debt, you may end up with bad credit.

THINGS TO CONSIDER BEFORE TAKING CREDIT

Borrowing needs careful thought and a strategy on how you will pay back the money you owe. Whether you are taking out a student loan or applying for a new credit card, you must give careful consideration to the reasons why you need credit. Financial literacy requires you to make conscious decisions when it comes to your finances. Without proper financial management, debt can turn into a gigantic mountain that stands between you and your dream life.

Before you apply for a loan, ask yourself the following.

• **What do you need credit for?** When taking out a loan, decide how much you need to borrow and be clear about how you intend to spend the money. This will allow you to use credit for its intended purpose and prevent you from using it on things you do not need. It will also help you decide on what type of loan to apply for.

• **How much will it cost?** Before applying for credit, always consider the annual percentage rate (APR), which is the cost of borrowing. You must know exactly how much the loan will cost you in total to ascertain whether you can afford it.

You also want to consider whether the interest rate is fixed or adjustable. Remember, by the time you are done paying back the loan, you will have paid more than the amount you borrowed. shop around for a better offer and ensure that you pay low interest rates.

If you are considering buying a product with a payment plan such as a mobile phone, ask yourself if it is worth paying interest on. Why not save for a few months and buy it in cash instead?

- **Can you afford the monthly payments?** Before committing to using borrowed funds, remember that you'll need to make monthly repayments. Can you afford the installment? Consider how much you earn and your other financial obligations to decide how much you can afford to pay back. This will help you decide how much you need to borrow.

- **What's your credit score?** Checking your credit score before applying for credit can help assess how you have managed debt in the past and whether you qualify. It also allows you to check if you need to raise your credit score. Some creditors charge lower interest rates if you have a good credit score.

- **How long will It take to pay off the debt?** Some credit terms and conditions may seem favorable and easy to pay off, but they are usually spread over a longer period of time which leads you to pay more in interest. Before making a commitment to paying for a television set over a three-year period, ask yourself if you were to lose your primary source of income, would you still be able to make those monthly installments?

- **Are there any financial fees?** Before applying for credit, first check what other fees apply. Some personal loan creditors charge an upfront sign-up fee which is deducted from your loan and used as a processing fee.

ADVANTAGES OF PAYING OFF DEBT ON TIME

Having a strategy for how you'll pay off your debt can prevent it from building up and help you avoid getting overwhelmed. Whenever you have extra funds to spare, pay off a little more than your usual monthly installment. It will reduce your credit balance, and before you know it, you'll have less debt to worry about.

Paying off your credit balance on time can save you money. For example, by paying off a personal loan on time you save on interest. The longer you take to pay off debt, the more you pay in interest.

Here are a few more reasons why you should pay off debt on time.

• **Improves your finances.** Paying off debt improves your finances. Once you stop paying debt, the money you were using to pay off debt can be diverted to your savings.

When you pay your debt on time, you become desirable to creditors who consider your debt-to-income ratio (the portion of your income that goes into debt repayment) to see if your income can cover loan repayments and that your current debt does not take up all your income. In other words, paying off debt on time improves your debt-to-income ratio and increases your chances of getting approved when applying for loans.

- **Reduces stress.** Paying off debt can be overwhelming, especially if you are paying off more than one debt, but it gives you a sense of relief and eases the pressure and stress of making those monthly payments. It gives you more control over your finances and peace of mind.

- **Improves your credit score.** Paying off your credit balance can also improve your credit score. Maxing out your credit limit lowers your credit score and may affect you when you want to take out credit in the future. Maintaining a good credit score puts you at an advantage with creditors.

AMORTIZING A LOAN

Loan amortization is the process of scheduling equal monthly payments that are applied to both the borrowed amount and the accumulated interest. The borrower pays off the interest for the period first and the remaining payment is made toward paying off the principal amount. More of each payment is channeled toward paying off the principal amount and less toward paying off the interest until the loan is paid off.

While loan amortization determines the minimum amount you have to pay each month toward your loan repayment, it does not prevent you from making additional payments. Any amount you pay that is above the minimum required amount is used to pay off the principal amount. This can help you save on interest over time.

Amortized loans include:

- personal loans
- home loans
- auto loans
- debt consolidation

Amortized Loans vs. Unamortized Loans

Amortized loan payments are spread out over the loan term. Since each payment is made toward the principal amount and the interest, amortized loan payments are usually higher than unamortized loan payments for the same principal amount and interest.

With an unamortized loan, you are required to pay interest during the loan term, and in some cases, you'll need to pay off the principal amount in full at the end of the loan term. Unamortized loan monthly payments are lower, however, making one full payment at the end of the loan term can be difficult. Instead of waiting until the end of the loan period to pay off the principal amount in full, you can make extra payments during the loan period which will be channeled toward paying off the principal amount.

Unamortized loans include:

- credit cards
- home equity lines of credit
- interest-only loans

- balloon payment loans, such as a mortgage

How an Amortized Loan Works

Loan amortization breaks down the loan amount into equal scheduled monthly payments. An amortization table is used to list each scheduled payment and how much goes into paying off the principal amount and paying off the interest. You can create your own amortization table, but the easiest way for a beginner is to use a template that will make calculations automatically.

An amortization table typically includes

- **Details of the loan.** Loan amortization calculations are based on the principal amount, loan period, and interest rate. If you are using an amortization calculator or table, you will use this information for your calculations.
- **Scheduled payments.** The first column in the amortization table usually lists how often you'll make payments. Monthly payments are the most common.
- **Principal repayment.** This part of the amortization table shows the amount you'll pay toward paying off the principal amount each month.
- **Interest.** The interest column shows the amount that goes into paying off the loan interest.

- **Extra payment.** If you make an extra payment above the required minimum monthly amount, the amortization calculator will apply the extra amount to the loan amount and calculate future interest payments based on the new loan balance.
- **Balance owing.** This column shows how much you still owe after each scheduled payment. It is calculated by deducting the principal amount paid in each period from the amount you currently owe.

Example of an Amortization Table

Say you took out a $25,000 auto loan with a five percent interest rate to be paid over a two-year period. Based on the amortization calculations below, you'd be required to pay $1,096.78 each month, with an initial monthly interest of $104,17. With time, your interest payment would decrease and you'd pay more toward the principal loan amount.

Below is an example of an amortization table. You can either create one yourself using a spreadsheet or use an online loan amortization calculator such as the one on www.thebalance-money.com to create your payment schedule.

Month	Initial Balance	Principal	Interest	Payment	Ending Balance
1	$20,000	$992.62	$104.17	$1,096.78	$24,007.38
2	$24,007.38	$996.75	$100.03	$1,096.78	$23,010.63
3	$23,010.63	$1,000.91	$95.88	$1,096.78	$22,009.72
4	$22,009.72	$1,005.08	$91.71	$1,096.78	$21,004.64
5	$21,004.64	$1,009.27	$87.52	$1,096.78	$19,995.38
6	$19,995.38	$1,013.47	$83.31	$1,096.78	$18,981.91
7	$18,981.91	$1,017.69	$79.09	$1,096.78	$17,964.21
8	$17,964.21	$1,021.93	$74.85	$1,096.78	$16,942.28
9	$16,942.28	$1,026.19	$70.59	$1,096.78	$15,916.09
10	$15,916.09	$1,030.47	$66.32	$1,096.78	$14,885.62
11	$14,885.62	$1,034.76	$62.02	$1,096.78	$13,850.86
12	$1,039.07	$1,039.07	$57.71	$1,096.78	$12,811.79
24	$1,092.23	$1,092.23	$4.55	$1,096.78	$0.00

BUILDING A STRONG FOUNDATION— UNDERSTANDING BANKING BASICS

A solid understanding of banking basics is the cornerstone of financial empowerment.

— UNKNOWN

W hether you choose to bank online or use a traditional bank or credit union, choosing the right bank account will ensure that your needs are met. Bank accounts provide security and convenience for your money, but they serve different purposes. Some are convenient for paying bills, while others are more inclined toward helping build your savings.

There are different types of bank accounts. These include:

- savings accounts
- checking accounts
- money market deposit accounts
- certificates of deposit (CD)
- individual retirement accounts (IRA)

Checking Account

A checking account is a type of bank account that you open with any bank, credit union, or online that you can use to deposit funds, transfer money in between accounts, and withdraw funds for your everyday expenses. This is the account you receive your paycheck into and pay your bills from, as well as keep funds that you can use at any time. Checking accounts save you from carrying cash around. All you need when going shopping is your debit card. When you swipe your card to pay for purchases, funds are immediately deducted from your account.

Checking accounts make paying bills and budgeting quite easy. They allow you to automate payments and pay your bills on time. All you need to do is set up the details of your bill as well as the date you'll make the payment. When the due date arrives, funds are deducted directly :from your account.

Other features of a checking account include:

- Direct deposits.
- Access to online banking through your bank's app or website.
- No minimum balance is needed to set up or maintain your account.

Banks and credit unions make money by charging fees. Before opening a checking account, find out the fees that apply to your bank account.

Common fees banks charge include:

- **Monthly maintenance fee.** Banks basically charge a fee to keep your money safe. Be clear about how much you'll pay each month to ensure that your account remains active.
- **Bank overdraft fees.** With a checking account, it is possible to spend more than your account balance, but your account will receive a penalty for overdrawn funds.
- **ATM fees.** With every ATM withdrawal you make, your bank charges you a transaction fee.
- **Bounced checks.** If you write a check and it is cashed in while you do not have funds in your account, you will be charged a fee for processing the bounced check.

Savings Account

A savings account is an account where you keep the money you don't intend to use immediately. Most savings accounts earn interest on deposits. The interest rate and annual percentage yield (APY) vary for different banks. Savings accounts usually have a minimum deposit amount. Check with the bank you intend to open a savings account with how much their minimum deposit fee is.

Different banks have different rules, and this applies to fees, as well. Some banks charge monthly maintenance fees on saving accounts while others do not have maintenance fees at all.

A savings account is designed to help you save money, which is why some do not come with a debit card. Another key feature of a savings account is that you can easily access your account online and transfer funds from your checking account. You may need to check with your bank first as most savings accounts limit the number of transfers and with-drawals you can make in a month. It's also important to note that the interest earned on a savings account is considered taxable income and must be included when filing tax returns.

Money Market Deposit Account

A money market deposit account is almost like a checking account and a savings account combined. It comes with a debit card and earns interest while keeping your money from the funds you use every day. If you want to open an emergency fund, a money market deposit account would be excellent for this purpose. You get to build your emergency fund separately from your checking account.

Like any other account, a money market account has its limits. For example, you may have a limit to the number of withdrawals and transfers you make each month. Also, there's a minimum balance and maintenance fee required to keep the account active.

Certificate of Deposit (CD)

A certificate of deposit account is an account where you keep your money for a specific period of time (known as the maturity term). During this time, your account earns interest, and once your CD maturity term expires, you can either withdraw your deposit together with the interest earned or carry over the balance to a new CD account.

CD accounts have different maturity terms with short-term accounts ranging from 12 months and below, mid-term accounts ranging from a year to three years, and long-term accounts ranging from four to five years. The longer you keep your money in your account, the higher your interest rate will be—usually one to two percent.

Though your interest rate will be higher than in a savings account, with CD accounts you cannot access your funds at any time. Withdrawing funds before the CD matures will attract a penalty.

Individual Retirement Account (IRA)

An individual retirement account is a great retirement savings strategy. There are different types of IRAs: a traditional IRA, a Roth IRA, a Savings Incentive Match Plan for Employees (SIMPLE), and a Simplified Employee Pension (SEP). Each has a different set of rules on taxation, withdrawals, and eligibility (Kagan,2022).

IRAs allow you to:

- contribute for as long as you have income from your job.
- continue making contributions even after retirement, as long as you earn income from a part-time job, but not your Social Security or pensions.
- have an individual account if you are married.

Individual retirement accounts are not like savings accounts. If you withdraw funds early, you will be charged a 10% withdrawal fee.

OPENING A BANK ACCOUNT

With advancements in technology, you no longer have to stand in a queue to be attended to by a bank teller. You can simply do your banking digitally through your mobile phone and save time. Online banking has made banking quite easy. Unless you prefer speaking to a banker, you can open an account with your chosen bank on your phone or computer through the bank's website.

If you don't have a bank account yet, here are the guidelines on how you can set one up.

Choose a Bank

If you have not decided on the type of bank you want to bank with, take some time to visit different banks or go through their websites to learn more about the products they offer. Comparing products from different banks can help you decide which bank will cater to your needs.

Visit the Bank or Their Website

The next step is to visit the bank with your identification documents and an initial deposit. For identification purposes, you will need to provide your:

- full name
- residential address
- date of birth
- identification number

You can also set up an account online by visiting your bank's website.

Choose the Type of Account You Want

As we discussed earlier, there are different bank account types and each has its own use. For example, if you want to focus more on your savings, a savings account would be a better option than a checking account. And, if you need an account to pay your bills and to receive your salary, a checking account would be more suitable.

Agree to the Terms and Conditions

Ensure that you read and understand the terms and conditions before signing the form. Most of the information on the form will be filled out for you. All you have to do is provide your documents and sign the form, and if you need clarity on any part of the form, ask your banker.

HOW TO WRITE A CHECK

Before you write a check, remember, it is not the quickest way to transfer funds. Also, ensure that you have funds in your checking account so your payments do not bounce and you incur penalties.

Once you have your checking account set up, here's how you can proceed to write your first check.

- **Fill in the date.** Write the date on the top right-hand corner of the check. This shows the bank and the person you are writing the check to when you wrote the check.
- **Write the payee's full name.** Where it is written "Pay to the order of," write the name of the person or company (known as the payee) you are writing the

check to. If you do not know the payee's name, you can write "Cash" on this part. This is risky because if you lose a check paid out to cash, anyone can deposit it.

- **Write the payment amount in numbers.** When filling out the payment amount, there are two spots you need to fill out. First, you must write the amount in numerical form in the box on the right-hand side of the check. For example, $510,36. Ensure that you write this figure clearly so the bank can deduct the correct amount from your account.

- **Write the payment amount in words.** Next, write the payment amount in words on the line below "Pay to the order of" and ensure that it matches the numerical amount. For example, if you are paying $510.36 you will write it as five hundred and ten and 36/100. If the payment amount is a whole number, still include 00/100 in the end for clarity. Writing the payment in words provides the bank with extra confirmation of the amount.

- **Write a memo.** Filling out this part of the check is optional, but it is helpful for remembering what you wrote the check for. For example, if you are writing a check for your rent, you can write "Monthly rent." Some companies may ask you to write your account number or invoice number on the memo line to ensure that payment is applied to the correct account.

- **Sign the check.** On the bottom right-hand corner of the check, sign your name using the signature you used to open your checking account. Your signature confirms to the bank that you agree to pay the payee the amount written on the check.

Security Tips

When filling out a check, be mindful of the following security tips to prevent fraud and bounced payments.

- Your signature must be consistent. Using the same signature can help you and your bank identify fraud. It makes it easier to prove that you did not sign a fraudulent check.
- Avoid writing a check to "Cash." If you lose the check, anyone can deposit it.
- To keep a record of all your checks, get a checkbook with carbon copies. They come with a thin sheet that has a copy of every check you write. This way, you'll have a record of all your payments.
- Write fewer checks. Remember there are alternative ways to make payments such as using your debit or credit card or cash, which are more convenient payment methods than writing a check. Instead of writing a check for your recurring bills, why not do an electronic transfer?

- Avoid blank checks. Writing a blank check gives the person you're writing the check to authorization to write any amount on the check.
- Use a dark pen when writing a check to ensure that it is readable and not easy to erase.

UNDERSTANDING YOUR BANK STATEMENT

A bank statement is a record of all your account transactions. It shows your account balance and the transactions you made over a set period, usually the last 30 days.

Your bank statement typically shows:

- Your name, bank account number (which appears as the last four digits of your account for security reasons), and mailing address.
- The period your statement covers—also known as the statement cycle.
- The bank's information such as phone number, website, and other relevant information such as how you can reach them if you have queries.
- A summary of all your transactions. You will see all your cash withdrawals, credits, purchases, and deposits made to your account.
- At the top of your transaction list, you'll see a detailed summary of your account with your starting balance,

- Your debits (funds you spent such as bill payments, and account fees), and credits (funds you received into your account such as your salary, or check deposits).
- The transaction date. Some transaction dates may reflect a day or two after you made the payment, usually on the day the bank processed the transaction.

ONLINE BANKING

Online banking has made transacting convenient. All you need is your smartphone or laptop and an internet connection to monitor your bank account and all your transactions.

Online banking gives you access to banking services from anywhere in the world without visiting your bank physically. You can transfer funds, pay your bills, and apply for a loan from your bank's mobile app. While online banking offers convenience when it comes to banking, you must know the pros and cons of using this banking service.

Advantages of Using Online Banking

- **Saves time.** With digital banking, you no longer have to visit a physical branch to do your banking, unless you'd like to speak to a banker in person. You have full access to your bank account on your bank's mobile app.

- **You can use the online banking service from anywhere.** Digital banking offers convenience. You can transfer funds, check your balance, and set up alerts for account overdrafts, all on your phone or laptop.
- **It's secure.** Financial institutions prioritize security. You can add multi factor authentication to your mobile app for extra verification. To add on, your funds are safe and insured by the Federal Deposit Insurance Corporation (FDIC).
- **You pay less fees.** Unlike physical banks, which charge monthly service fees for accounts, online banks tend to charge minimum fees on accounts.
- **It's easy to use.** And it is a fast way to make transfers and pay your bills.

Disadvantages of Using Online Banking

- **Lack of personal relationships.** While online banks have a customer service department where you can contact the bank if you have any queries, the experience is not the same as speaking to a banker at a physical bank. Bankers are motivated to help clients and build ties with them in order to retain them.
- **Technology disruption.** If your internet service is down or there's site maintenance you will not have

access to your account until the system is up and running again.

- **Offers limited services.** With online banks, you may not have access to other financial services that physical banks offer, such as insurance. Online banks also do not offer notarization and signature guarantee services to authenticate your signature.
- **Privacy and security concerns.** While online banks update their servers from time to time and ensure security measures are in place to protect users, if your account is hacked you are at risk of identity theft. Using insecure networks also puts you at risk of having your login credentials stolen.

Online Banking Features

Most online banks offer as many features as banking in person. You can:

- access your deposit and account history;
- view your e-statements and account balance;
- link your debit card to your PayPal account;
- reorder checks; and,
- transfer funds between accounts.

Is Online Banking Safe?

Online banks and credit unions have policies in place to ensure customer accounts are protected. They use website encryptions, fraud monitoring, and firewalls on their computers as security measures. However, this does not mean you should let down your guard as an account holder. You must be alert and ensure that your account is protected at all times.

Here's how you can keep your account protected when using online banking.

- **Do not share your account details with anyone.** Be wary of emails or phone calls that request your confidential information. Your bank will not call or email you asking for your details. Also, use your login details only on the official bank site—which should and must be a secure site.
- **Change your password often.** The first time you use online banking services, you will use the login credentials the bank gives you. It's advisable to change this password after your first login to protect your account. You can change the password regularly and protect your login details always.
- **Check your bank statement often.** While banks have measures in place that detect fraud, it's important to check your bank statement often to make sure there are no fraudulent transactions.
- **Avoid using public computers and Wi-Fi.** When using online banking, avoid using public computers. You risk having your login credentials traced or seen by people. If you have to use a public computer or

Wi-Fi, ensure that you clear the browsing history from the computer after using it.

- **Disconnect your internet if you're not using it.** Leaving your computer connected to the Internet always can be risky. Hackers can access it through your internet connection. Ensure that your Wi-Fi is password protected, or disconnect your internet if you're not using it.

- **Use a licensed anti-virus software.** Purchase a licensed anti-virus software and keep it updated to protect your computer. Using a pirated version may come for free, but it does not provide complete protection from viruses and malware.

- **Type your bank's URL.** Avoid clicking on URLs sent to your email even if they look legitimate. Fraudsters have a tendency to send emails that contain a URL that may look like your bank's website. When you use that website, they can gain access to your account details and wipe out your funds. Instead, when logging into your account, type your bank's URL and ensure that it's correct.

- **Enable multi-factor authentication (MFA).** Multi-factor authentication provides added security when login into your account. Each time you login to your account, the bank will require additional information to verify it's you. This can be in the form of a unique code sent to your mobile number or your fingerprint. Multi-factor authentication provides added protection to your account, making it less likely for anyone to easily access your account.

BASICS OF USING AN ATM

Automated teller machines (ATMs) allow you to deposit and withdraw money from your account. You can find ATMs inside and outside a bank, and in busy places such as shopping centers, gas stations, airports, and restaurants.

To withdraw cash from an ATM, follow the steps below.

1. Locate a nearby ATM using Google or mapping software.
2. Check your surroundings to ensure you're safe.
3. Insert your card into the ATM with the card's chip facing forward.
4. Select your language.
5. Enter your personal identification number (PIN) when prompted.
6. On the screen, you'll see different transaction types such as deposits, withdrawals, and transfers. Select the transaction type you want to perform.
7. Select "withdrawal" under transaction type.
8. Select the account you want to withdraw funds from.
9. Enter your withdrawal amount and ensure it does not exceed your account balance.
10. Take your card back and wait for your cash to be processed.

To deposit a check or cash into an ATM affiliated with your bank follow the steps below.

1. Select deposit on step 6 and choose the account you're depositing into.
2. Enter the deposit amount.
3. Next, select "cash," "checks," or "cash and checks" if the ATM has this option.
4. Insert your money or check into the designated slot.
5. Confirm your deposit.
6. Remove your debit card and take your receipt.

OVERDRAFT PROTECTION

Overdraft protection is an agreement financial institutions make with their clients to allow transactions to exceed the balance in their checking accounts. This means you can process transactions even if you have insufficient funds in your account and the bank will cover the overdraft so the transaction goes through. To use the overdraft protection service, the bank will either charge you a fee each time you use the service or a fixed monthly fee.

Processing transactions with insufficient funds in your account results in bounced checks and declined debit transactions. This can be costly because the bank will charge you a penalty fee for declined transactions due to insufficient funds.

To avoid overdraft fees, link your checking account to a savings account or credit card that will kick in when you exceed your checking account balance. This will apply when you write a check, make a wire transfer, or withdraw cash from an ATM for an amount above your available balance. Funds will be transferred from the linked account to cover the shortfall when the overdraft protection service is activated.

Advantages of Using the Overdraft Protection Service

- The recipient will not be notified that you have insufficient funds in your account to make payment.
- Your transaction is guaranteed to go through.
- It helps you avoid overdraft fees. If you're unaware of your account balance, you'll be charged overdraft fees for every declined transaction.
- You pay less in fees. The overdraft protection service fee is typically lower than an overdraft fee.
- You are covered during emergencies. Even with an insufficient balance, you can have access to funds.

Disadvantages of Using the Overdraft Protection Service

- Banks can cancel the overdraft protection service at any time, especially if your account balance remains negative for quite some time.
- You could be tempted to spend more and develop the habit of spending money you do not have.

- If you do not have sufficient funds on your linked accounts, your transactions will be declined.
- You may still be charged overdraft fees. Some banks charge a fee if you have multiple overdraft transactions.
- If you manage your funds well and never use the overdraft protection service, the bank will still charge you a service fee.

The Overdraft Protection Trap

While overdraft protection can get your transactions approved—even if you have insufficient funds in your account if you are not cautious, the service can leave you in serious debt. Some banks will make it easy to have access to overdraft protection services if they believe you are credit-worthy. But, they do not limit access to the service if you are having financial difficulties. This leads most people who are already facing financial difficulties to fall into the overdraft debt trap.

Each month an overdraft is not paid off, your account balance sinks deeper into debt as overdraft fees accumulate on top of the balance you owe. A service that is intended to help you get through financial difficulties ends up driving you into more problems.

How to Avoid Overdraft Fees

Managing your finances and ensuring that your account balance is always positive is the best way to avoid overdraft fees. But, if you do spend more than what is in your account there are ways you can avoid paying hefty overdraft fees.

- **Cancel the Overdraft Protection Service.** You can choose to opt out of the overdraft protection service. This means your bank will only be covering checks and recurring debit transactions and not one-time debit and ATM transactions. Without the overdraft protection service, your bank cannot process transactions if you do not have enough funds in your account, therefore you will not incur overdraft fees.
- **Monitor your account balance.** Check your account balance regularly and ensure that it is positive, especially if you have inconsistent income.
- **Link your checking account to your savings account or line of credit.** When you don't have enough funds in your checking account to process a transaction, funds will be deducted from your linked account to cover the shortfall. Before linking a different account to your checking account, find out the fees associated with the service from your bank. You may be charged transfer fees.
- **Quickly make a deposit when an overdraft occurs.** Check if your bank has a cut-off time that allows you to add funds to your account. When you receive an

overdraft notification, immediately deposit or transfer funds into your checking account to prevent other fees, such as a continuous negative balance fee.

- **Find a bank with a better overdraft policy.** Some banks only charge overdraft fees when you reach a certain amount. Others give you a cut-off time and do not charge a fee as long as you transfer funds into your account as soon as an overdraft occurs.
- **Use a prepaid debit card.** With prepaid debit cards you can deposit and withdraw funds as well as set a spending limit. Prepaid debit cards are not linked to your checking account and they do not have overdraft services, but they do have a fee for declined transactions.

Understanding the fundamentals of banking puts you ahead of the financial game. It allows you to make smart financial decisions, pick the right financial institution to do business with that will cater to your needs, and choose financial products that align with your financial goals.

Whether you choose to bank with a traditional bank or opt for a digital bank, ensure that you understand the pros and cons of each and the products they offer.

While your bank may have security measures in place to protect your account, remember to keep your sensitive information and login credentials to your account safe to prevent getting hacked. Always take precautions and keep your account protected at all times.

With the right financial tools, you can set yourself up for a bright future. You can start saving for your college fund and planning your career path.

While deciding what career path to take can be overwhelming, there are some guidelines that can help you decide on a career that suits you. We'll learn more about those next.

8

COLLEGE EDUCATION—NOT ALL PATHS ARE THE SAME

Education is the most powerful weapon which you can use to change the world.

— NELSON MANDELA

College life can be an exciting experience. Not only does it provide you with an opportunity to broaden your horizons, but it also gives you the opportunity to meet new people and expand your social circle. However, the transition from high school to college is a big change for students. Like any other major life transition, this new chapter of your life needs preparation—both emotionally and financially—especially if you'll be moving away from home for the first time.

Understanding what's ahead and preparing yourself for this new chapter of your life can make the transition less stressful.

Before we dive into how to pick a good college and what to expect, you should understand that higher education is not only limited to universities and four-year colleges. There are alternative colleges that are as good as four-year colleges that will cater to your career goals and interests.

TYPES OF HIGHER EDUCATION

Public and Private Universities

Public universities are local or state government-funded educational institutions that offer low tuition rates to in-state residents. They allow out-of-state students, but they often pay higher tuition fees. Public universities offer a wide range of courses and often have large student bodies. There's at least one public university in each state in the United States, which makes accessing college education affordable to students.

Private colleges and universities are higher education institutions that are mainly funded through endowments, donations, and tuition fees from private sources. These private sources could be individuals or organizations. Private universities tend to have a smaller student population and often have higher tuition fees, but offer financial aid to qualifying students.

Colleges

Colleges are smaller institutions that offer students a wide variety of subjects instead of specializing in one subject. These include liberal arts colleges which are four-year undergraduate institutions that mainly focus on arts, sciences, social science, and humanities. Liberal arts colleges offer students a wide variety of subjects to help them develop their critical thinking skills.

Community Colleges

Often, when students are not sure of what path to take after high school, they take courses at a community college to help them carve out a career path and define their career goals.

Community colleges are affordable and they offer a two-year associate's degree that prepares students for the job market after graduation.

Most of the time the credits from community college courses can be transferred to a four-year university degree program—saving you money on tuition.

Technical Institutes

Also known as institutes of technology, technical institutes provide education on technology systems. They provide research and vocational training and offer programs such as computer science, medical information technology, electronics, and health sciences—designed to prepare students for practical application-based careers.

Online Degrees

Online degree programs have become a norm. This is partly because they offer the flexibility to study from anywhere. An online degree curriculum is often the same as an on-campus curriculum. Students who study online degrees earn the same degree as on-campus students.

Online learning is not for all students, which is why most traditional colleges offer both on-campus learning and distance learning.

COLLEGE COSTS

When planning for college, take into consideration all of the costs involved so you can fully prepare yourself. Create a realistic list of your expenses and leave out everything else you may not need.

Here's a list of common college expenses and how you can minimize them. You can personalize the list and add other expenses as you see fit.

- **Tuition.** Research different institutions and choose an affordable college that meets your needs.
- **Live at home.** Instead of renting an apartment, live at home and save on rent.
- **Equipment.** A laptop and printer are among the essential pieces of equipment you'll need. Shop around for the best deal and also consider refurbished computers. They are very affordable.
- **Personal expenses.** You'll need to budget for essentials such as clothing, toiletries, cosmetics, a phone bill, health insurance, and medical supplies. You may also want to cook your meals at home and save on takeout.

- **School supplies.** Consider buying used books to save money, or rent books on sites such as Amazon and eCampus.
- **Transportation.** If you commute daily, use public transportation. It's a much more affordable option than driving, which will require you to pay for gas, insurance, and maintenance.
- **School and activity fees.** Before you enroll in a college, check what your total annual fees would be. Also, note that some classes with labs may have additional fees.

SAVING FOR COLLEGE

Developing responsible spending habits earlier on gives you a good head start financially. It teaches you to manage your finances as well as find ways to supplement your income. With good money management skills, you may be able to pay off your student loans or put a down payment on a home immediately after graduation.

Financial goals differ for everyone and needs and wants vary from person to person. Keep this in mind when deciding what your essentials are for college and what you can do without.

Here are a few ways you can start saving for college and preparing for your future.

- **Open a College Savings Account.** A 529 plan offers tax-free growth and withdrawals, and is an excellent way to save for your educational costs.
- **Use a Roth IRA.** After the Roth IRA has been funded for five years, you can withdraw up to $10,000 in earnings tax and penalty-free. Roth IRA earnings can be used for qualified education expenses, such as college tuition and school supplies (O'Shea and Taube, 2023).
- **Cut down on senior year expenses.** Utilize student discounts and cut down on expenses. StudentRate.com often lists discounts on textbooks, laptops, clothes, and loads of other stuff.
- **Consider attending community college.** Community college can be a great foundation for your education. It is much more affordable than most colleges and you can still enroll at a four-year university afterward.
- **Get a part-time job.** Campuses often have job openings for students. You could get a job in the campus library, for instance. Or, as an administrative assistant. Also, consider enrolling in a work-study program that could allow you to pay your tuition through the campus job.

COLLEGE SCHOLARSHIPS AND GRANTS

Grants and scholarships are similar. They both offer financial aid to students, and unlike loans, do not need to be repaid. Grants are offered by large institutions such as the federal government, the state, and colleges.

Students with a particular set of skills often qualify for multiple scholarships. When applying for a student grant or scholarship, remember, both are highly competitive. To increase your chances of being accepted, submit your application early.

• **College-based grants.** Most colleges offer financial aid to low-income students. Grants can also be given to students based on merit or field of study. For example, athletic grants are awarded to students with a high-grade point average (GPA) and athletic talent.

• **State-sponsored grants.** These are directly awarded through state-sponsored programs or directly by colleges. These grants provide funding to students from minority demographics or in high-demand fields. Some colleges consider characteristics such as gender, ethnicity, and intended area of study.

There are state-sponsored grants awarded to students based on merit that look at a student's GPA and standardized test scores. Other grants are awarded based on a student's membership or involvement in the state organization.

- **Federal grants.** The U.S. Department of Education offers a wide range of federal grants to students attending four-year colleges or universities, community colleges, and career schools. The most common federal government funding is the Pell Grant.

The Pell Grant is usually given to students whose families earn an income of less than $20,000 (Scholarships.com, n.d.-a). Qualifying students who receive a Pell Grant can still apply for other federal grants, such as the Federal Supplemental Educational Opportunity Grant (FSEOG).

- **Student-specific grants.** Student grants are available for students who meet different criteria. Whether you come from a low-income family or are returning to school, there are grants for your specific situation.

Most grants are need-based. You must fill out a Free Application for Federal Student Aid (FAFSA) to determine your need. Other grants are merit-based and award students with a high GPA. Make a list of your skills and qualities and check organizations, private corporations, and local groups that have funding programs for your skill set.

- **Career-specific grants.** Career-specific grants are popular in fields such as teaching and nursing. The federally-funded Teacher Education Assistance for College and Higher Education (TEACH) grant provides funding for teaching students who plan to work in low-income school districts. The U.S. Department of Health and Human Services pays tuition and fees for nursing students through the Nursing Scholarship Program in exchange for two years of service at facilities with a nursing shortage. Choosing a high-demand field can help pay for your education expenses.

PAYING COLLEGE FEES (PARENT'S GUIDE)

For most parents, preparing for their child's college education is both an exciting and emotional experience. Seeing your child grow and finally gain independence is every parent's dream. However, if you're not financially prepared, this could be an extremely emotional time—especially if you have more than one child. Fortunately, there are ways you can start saving early for your child's college education and avoid getting into debt.

- **Take advantage of educational tax benefits** such as the Lifetime Learning Tax Credit (LLTC), which you can claim when you file your federal income tax returns—based on how much you paid for college expenses (Kantrowitz, 2022). You can also take a tax deduction on student loans you take out for your child's higher education.
- **Invite others to help.** Invite friends and family members to make small contributions for special occasions such as birthdays or holidays to a 529 account. Most 529 plans accept gifts. For example,

Ascensus has a 529 gift plan called Ugift that allows account owners to receive contributions.

- **Invest in a 529 account.** This is an effective way to start saving for your child's higher education. The 529 plan is a state-sponsored investment plan to pay for future education expenses. They're usually tax-friendly, and if you use the funds for qualified education expenses you won't have to pay taxes on your earnings.

- **Open a Coverdell education savings account.** According to the IRS, the Coverdell Education Savings Account (Coverdell ESA) is a trust account that can be used to pay for elementary, secondary, and higher education expenses. You can only contribute up to $2,000 for each beneficiary every year. Contributions are nondeductible and must be made in cash. The distributions from a Coverdell (ESA) are tax-free as long as the distributions don't exceed the beneficiary's qualified education expenses.

- **Invest in savings bonds.** Investing into eligible savings bonds is a low-risk education savings plan. The interest earned from savings bonds is free from state and local income taxes, but federal taxes do apply when the bond matures, when you redeem it, or when it stops earning interest. Savings bonds have a low return on investment (ROI) and can take up to

20 years to mature. Once redeemed, the funds can be used for higher education expenses.

- **Invest in Mutual Funds.** Mutual funds are not designed specifically for paying for college, but are rather meant to diversify your investment portfolio and create passive income. Do keep in mind that earnings from mutual funds are taxable, and capital gains will be taxed when you sell your shares. This could affect your child's eligibility for financial aid.

- **Contribute to a Roth IRA.** A Roth IRA is a tax-advantaged individual retirement account you can contribute after-tax dollars into. There is no immediate tax deduction or other tax benefit for contributing to the account. Once your account is funded, you can invest that money through the Roth IRA, and over time, your investment is likely to earn a return.

- **Take out a home-equity loan.** Home-equity loans often have lower interest rates than student loans, which could save you money over the duration of the loan. If you're looking to fund your child's higher education, a home equity loan may be an option. But, before taking out a home equity loan, consider saving for college, applying for scholarships, and choosing an affordable school, because if you fail to make payments toward your home equity loan, you could face foreclosure.

Once your child starts sending out college applications, it's advisable to fill out the Free Application for Federal Student Aid (FAFSA). Most students are eligible for scholarships, grants, student loans, and work-study programs. Ensure that you fill out the FAFSA form each year your child is in college, as most institutional scholarships require the FAFSA form to be on file.

STUDENT LOANS

Student loans are the most common form of funding for college education. There are two types of student loans: federal and private. Federal student loans are the most common form of financial aid for higher education in the U.S., partly because they have lower interest rates and better terms than private student loans. Each type of loan has its own advantages and disadvantages. Before deciding on a loan, consider all your options to ascertain whether the loan you're applying for is suitable for your circumstances.

To apply for federal student loans, you must fill in the Free Application for Federal Student Aid (FAFSA) form each year you're in college. You can complete the form online at FAFSA.com or use the myStudentAid mobile app.

Types of Student Loans

• **Direct subsidized loan.** Direct subsidized loans are offered to undergraduate students with a financial need. Compared to other federal student loans, this loan has better terms because the federal government covers the interest during certain periods, including during the six-month grace period you're given after you leave college.

Direct subsidized loans have several repayment plans that are designed to help you if you're struggling financially. You do not have to repay the loan while you are still in school and during a six-month grace period after leaving college.

• **Direct unsubsidized loans.** Unsubsidized loans are given to qualifying undergraduate and graduate students and are not financial need-based. With this type of loan, you are responsible for the interest that accrues during the loan term and the period in which the loan is not in active repayment.

Like subsidized loans, you do not have to repay direct unsubsidized loans while you are still in school and during a six-month grace period after leaving school; but, your interest accumulates and you'll be required to pay it when your loan repayment schedule begins.

• **Direct consolidation loans.** Consolidation loans allow borrowers to combine all qualifying federal student loans into a single loan. This is usually done after leaving school. Consolidating your loans makes it easier to manage repayments. Paying a single and possibly lower monthly payment and one student loan servicer is less overwhelming than paying several debts.

• **Direct PLUS loans.** A Direct PLUS Loan is a federal loan from the Department of Education given to students known as a Grad PLUS loan or their parents (Parent PLUS loan) to help them cover education expenses after they've exhausted private loans. A credit check is required to acquire a Direct PLUS Loan; however, borrowers with a bad credit history can still obtain a PLUS loan with a co-signer.

With a Parent PLUS loan, your parents can only take out a loan that covers the cost of attendance determined by your school. The terms of these loans are often less favorable, which is why you should consider direct subsidized and unsubsidized loans first.

With the Grad PLUS loan, you do not have to make payments while still in school. You can apply for an income-driven repayment plan after leaving college, but interest does accumulate.

Parent PLUS loans are not eligible for an income-driven payment plan, but your parents can request a deferment if they need to as long as you remain in school—at least half-time. The repayment schedule begins six months after graduating or dropping out of school.

- **Health professional student loans**. Health professional student loans are available to students studying in the field of medicine, such as nursing, sports medicine, dentistry, and veterinary medicine. There are four types of health profession loans offered by the U.S. government to students at participating schools who demonstrate a financial need.

238 | GEORGIA I. LAINIOTIS, MBA, MA

- Primary Care Loans (PCL)
- Nursing School Loans (NSL)
- Loans for Disadvantaged Students (LDS)
- Health Professions Student Loans (HPSL)

Each loan has its own eligibility requirements. To learn more about health professional student loans, visit the Health Resources and Services Administration (HRSA) website.

• **Undergraduate loans.** Unlike federal student loans, undergraduate private student loans often require a co-signer. The co-signer must be an adult who agrees to take responsibility if you fail to repay your loans. Private lenders often require co-signers since most undergraduates don't have a credit history.

• **Graduate loans.** Private lenders sometimes offer student loans to students in specific schools such as graduate school, medical school, business school, and law school. Private loans for graduate or professional students often have higher loan limits, longer repayment terms, and lower interest rates, and are less likely to require a co-signer. In some cases, private lenders may give you a longer grace period and in-school deferment periods while you complete your studies.

FEDERAL LOANS VS. PRIVATE LOANS

Most student loans are acquired through the William D. Ford Federal Direct Loan Program. In cases where a student requires additional financial aid to complete their college education, they often turn to private lenders, such as banks or credit unions.

There are notable differences between federal student loans and private student loans. These include the cost of repayment and the credit score requirement in ascertaining whether you qualify for the loan.

Another difference between the two loans is that undergraduate students applying for federal loans do not go through a credit check, whereas graduate students applying for the same loan must go through a credit check, and if their credit history isn't so good, their loan application can be rejected.

A credit score of 640 or above is usually required. Depending on the terms and conditions of the loan, a higher score may be needed for your loan application to be approved.

Other differences between federal and private student loans include:

- Federal student loans have fixed interest rates which are lower than that of private student loans. Interest rates on private student loans can be variable or fixed.
- You don't have to repay federal loans until you graduate or drop below half-time student status.

Most private lenders require you to repay the student loan while enrolled in school.

- Federal student loans are subsidized; meaning, the government pays your interest while you're still in school. With private student loans, you pay the interest yourself.
- Federal loans have flexible repayment plans and loan forgiveness programs whereas private loans only have a few repayment options and no loan forgiveness programs.

Which Type of Student Loan Should You Choose?

There are no fixed rules for deciding which loan type is suitable for you. It partly depends on your financial situation and risk tolerance. But, in general, consider the federal student loan as the first option.

Federal student loans offer different repayment options, loan forgiveness programs, and longer deferment periods than private loans. They don't have a minimum credit score requirement, which makes them accessible to undergraduates without the need to have a cosigner.

In cases where a student does not qualify for a federal student loan because of citizenship status or if they need more financial aid than what federal loans offer, private student loans are the best option. Additionally, if you have a good credit score, a private student loan could be a better option. You could get lower starting rates from a private lender than the federal government.

CONSOLIDATING YOUR STUDENT LOANS

Student loan consolidation is the process of combining all your federal student loans into one loan. You can apply for a federal student loan consolidation through the U.S. Department of Education's Federal Student Aid office—free of charge. Consolidating your student loans does not necessarily lower your interest rate, but it reduces your monthly payment.

If you have defaulted on one or more federal student loans, you can use consolidation as an alternative to loan rehabilitation.

You can consolidate most federal student loans, but not private student loans. With private student loans, you can combine them into one, new, private loan together with federal student loans in a process known as student loan refinancing.

Like any other loan, a consolidated student loan has its own pros and cons. Before consolidating your loans, make sure that you understand what the advantages and disadvantages are.

242 | GEORGIA I. LAINIOTIS, MBA, MA

CONSOLIDATION VS. REFINANCING

Student loan consolidation allows you to combine all your federal student loans into a single loan. While consolidating your loans simplifies the loan repayment process and enables you to pay low monthly payments, you're likely to pay more interest over time. This means that it's not the best way to save money. Instead, the process only prolongs your repayment period.

Student loan refinancing, on the other hand, allows you to pay lower interest rates, which saves you money over the loan term. However, refinancing student loans with one private loan means you won't have repayment options or access to federal loan protections and forgiveness programs.

Advantages of Consolidating Student Loans

- It will be easier to manage your debt and choose a repayment plan that is best for your financial situation.
- You get a longer repayment term.
- You can switch from a variable to a fixed-rate loan.
- It allows you to pay less in monthly installments.
- You can alternate repayment options, including income-driven (IDR) plans.

Disadvantages of Consolidating Your Student Loans

- A longer repayment term means you'll pay more interest over time.
- Accrued interest on individual loans is included in the consolidated loan principal.
- You'll no longer have access to benefits such as loan cancellation on certain loans and discounted rates.
- You'll be unable to pay off individual loans to lower your monthly installment.
- You'll lose credit for any pre-consolidation payments toward Public Service Loan Forgiveness (PSLF) or an IDR plan.

GETTING APPROVED FOR STUDENT LOAN CONSOLIDATION

You can consolidate your federal student loans when you graduate, are no longer enrolled in school, or drop out below half-time student status. There's no credit check required to consolidate federal student loans. However, there are other requirements that qualify students for a direct consolidation loan.

To be eligible for a student loan consolidation you need to consider the following:

- The loans you want to consolidate must be in repayment or in a grace period.

- You can't consolidate an existing consolidation loan unless you include an additional qualifying loan in the consolidation.
- If you want to consolidate a defaulted loan, you must either:
- make three consecutive monthly payments on the loan before you consolidate; or,
- repay your consolidated loan under an income-driven repayment plan.

How Long Does Student Loan Consolidation Take?

Completing the direct consolidation loan application takes about 30 minutes. It usually takes four to six weeks for your loan consolidation to be completed after submitting the relevant paperwork.

Your loan servicer will give you details of your loan repayment including when the first payment on the consolidated loan is due. If you can, immediately set up an automatic payment method to avoid missing payments. If you don't receive a response on your loan consolidation application within the specified time period, continue to make payments on your existing loans until you do to avoid paying late fees.

Which Student Loans Are Eligible for Consolidation?

Student loans eligible for consolidation include:

- direct subsidized loans
- direct unsubsidized loans
- direct PLUS loans
- parent loans for undergraduate students
- federal Perkins loans
- health education assistance loans
- nursing student loans
- nurse faculty loans
- health professions student loans
- FFEL PLUS loans

HOW TO CONSOLIDATE FEDERAL STUDENT LOANS

To consolidate your federal student loan, log in to the Federal Financial Aid (FSA) website. You can view your loan details and complete a consolidation application and promissory note. The promissory note is the promise you make to the loan servicer to repay the loan.

To consolidate your federal student loans, follow the steps below.

1. Log into your federal aid account. Use the login details you signed up with to sign in at studentaid.gov. Select the "Manage Loans" button, and then select "Consolidate Loans."

2. Prepare the relevant documents. If you're completing the application online, you'll have access to all of your federal loan details. You must provide contact information for two people who have known you for at least three years—it could be your parent or legal guardian.

3. Fill in a consolidation loan application. Next, complete a Direct Consolidation Loan Application and Promissory Note. This free application includes the following sections:

a. **Choose a loan and servicer.** On the first section of the loan application, you'll be required to select the loans you want to consolidate. The site will calculate your loans and the new consolidated loan amount and interest rate. You can also choose a loan servicer in this section—as well as request a grace period.

b. **Choose repayment.** Repayment options depend on the types of loans you're consolidating and your financial status. Your estimated monthly payments are calculated in this section—under several plans using your income, tax status, and family size. Next, you'll be asked to choose a repayment plan.

c. **Terms and conditions.** This section of the application states the terms and conditions of the new consolidated federal loan. This is where you'll establish your understanding of the agreement and agree to pay the consolidated loan.

d. **Personal information.** In this section, you'll fill in all your details, including your residential address, driver's license number, contact information, and employer details. Next, you'll provide the details of your two contact people.

e. Review and sign. Lastly, review your application and acknowledge that all the information you provided is true and correct, and that you understand the repayment terms and conditions—and sign the form.

4. Await approval. At the end of the application process, you'll receive the loan servicer's contact information. The loan approval process usually takes between 30 and 90 days and depends on the servicer. Once your application is approved, the lender will pay the balance on your student loans with your direct consolidation loan.

5. Start the repayment process. Your repayment amount and schedule will depend on the repayment plan you chose during the application process. The loan servicer will inform you of your payment schedule and when you need to make your first payment.

ARE THERE ALTERNATIVES TO STUDENT LOAN CONSOLIDATION?

For students who do not want to consolidate their loans, there are other options that can help you pay off your student loans. These include deferment, forbearance, and IDR plans—designed for students struggling to make their monthly payments.

- **Deferment.** Student loan deferment allows you to pause your payments for a certain period. Interest on subsidized federal student loans or Perkins loans does not accrue during the deferment period.
- **Forbearance.** If you do not qualify for deferment, you can apply for forbearance. You'll be allowed to pause payments for 12 months, but you're responsible for paying the accrued interest on all your federal loans.
- **Income-driven repayment plan (IDR).** Income-driven repayment (IDR) options allow you to lower your monthly payments based on your income. Monthly payments are usually between 10% and 20% of your monthly discretionary income (the income amount left after paying for all your necessities).
- **Private refinancing.** If you want to pay a lower interest rate or want to consolidate private student loans, refinancing would be a better option.

There are so many ways you can fund your college education. Whether you want to attend a technical or community college, picking the right institution can help you achieve your career goals.

I hope by now I've inspired you and that you're excited about your future. There's no limit to how far you can go in life. We live in a world filled with vast knowledge to help us succeed in life. What you need is a curious, open mind that is ready to learn. Next, we'll learn how to build wealth long-term through investments and why building your investment portfolio early is important.

9

UNDERSTANDING THE BASICS OF INVESTING

It's not how much money you make, but how much money you keep, how hard it works for you, and how many generations you keep it for.

— ROBERT KIYOSAKI

Both saving and investing are key to building a solid financial foundation. They go hand in hand, but they are not the same. While both can help you achieve financial freedom, there are key differences between the two concepts.

First, let's define the two concepts to gain a better understanding of how they work. Saving is putting money aside for a specific purpose. For example, saving for a vacation or saving up for emergencies. To save money, you need to put it into cash products, such as a savings account or credit union.

On the contrary, investing is taking a portion of your money and using it to buy products or assets that might increase in value in the long run. For example, investing in stocks, real estate, or buying shares in a fund.

The main difference between saving and investing is the level of risk involved. Saving often has a lower return with no risk. Investing, on the other hand, gives you the opportunity to earn a higher return, but the risk of losing your capital is higher.

INVESTING EXPLAINED

An investment is an asset or product acquired with the assumption that it will increase in value, produce income, or both. For example, buying equity stock of a listed company with the hope that the share price will increase and you'll receive regular dividends in the future.

The main reason for investing is to have your money work for you so you can invest in more income-generating assets. When it comes to investing, keep in mind that there's always an element of risk associated with any investment.

There are two types of investments:

1. **Fixed-income investments.** These are investments that pay investors a fixed income; for example, government and corporate bonds.
2. **Variable-income investments.** These are investments with a rate of return that changes and is determined by market forces. Variable-income investments include stocks and shares, have a higher risk, and can produce potentially greater rewards.

INVESTMENT IDEAS FOR TEENS

There are endless opportunities to invest your money and watch it grow over time. While the world of investments is quite broad, there are common types of investments people use to appreciate their capital.

• **Stocks.** Also known as equities, stocks are ownership of shares in a company. When you own a company's stock, you become a fractional owner of that company and can participate in its growth. Stockholders receive regular dividends paid out of the company's profits when the company's share price appreciates.

• **Bonds.** A bond is a debt security issued by entities such as governments, municipalities, and corporations. These entities issue bonds to raise funds from investors who are willing to lend them money for a certain period of time. In return, the issuer will pay you interest during the life of the bond and when the bond matures, you'll receive the capital you invested into the bond back.

• **Mutual Funds and Exchange-Traded Funds (ETFs).** A mutual fund is a pool of money from many investors that is invested in securities such as stocks, bonds, shares, commodities, and short-term debt. The most common types of funds are mutual funds and ETFs. When you buy shares in a mutual fund you become part-owner in the fund and the income it generates.

Instead of investing in individual companies, mutual funds often combine specific investments into one investment vehicle. For example, instead of researching and buying shares from individual companies, you can buy shares of a single mutual fund that owns different companies.

• **Options and other derivatives.** Options are popular derivatives that get their value from an underlying asset such as a stock, commodity, or bond. They're a contract to exchange an asset; for example, a share of stock at a specified price in the future. Options trading is highly speculative, and options are often used as leverage. This allows traders to buy more stock with less money and increase their returns, but at the same time makes them a high-risk, high-reward investment.

• **Commodities.** These are raw materials used in the production of goods and services. They include agricultural products, mineral ores, and fossil fuels. Commodities can be traded through ETFs or commodity futures (an agreement to buy or sell a commodity at a specified price on a future date). There are four types of commodities:

- **Energy.** This includes oil, natural gas, ethanol, coal, and uranium, as well as forms of renewable energy such as solar power.
- **Agricultural products.** These include goods such as grain, sugar, cocoa, soybeans, coffee, and wheat.
- **Livestock.** Livestock includes all live animals, such as cows and sheep.

- **Metals.** These include gold, silver, copper, aluminum, platinum, palladium, iron ore, tin, and zinc.

- **Real Estate Investment Trusts (REIT).** A real estate investment trust (REIT) is a company that owns and operates income-producing real estate or related assets. Similar to mutual funds, REITs pool capital from a number of investors, allowing individual investors to earn dividends from real estate investments, without buying, managing, or financing any properties themselves.

REITs allow individuals to invest in large-scale, income-generating real estate such as office buildings, apartments, hotels, resorts, warehouses, self-storage facilities, and shopping malls.

WHY INVEST?

Investing your money is important for a couple of reasons. It allows you to create wealth in the long run. To build wealth, you must have different avenues that generate a consistent income for you.

While saving can help you achieve some of your short-term financial goals, such as buying a car, investing allows you to achieve your long-term financial goals, such as saving for retirement.

- It allows you to earn compound interest on your investments, which increases your returns.
- Additionally, the more streams of income you have the better the chances you have of surviving unexpected life events such as a job loss when they hit you.
- Investing also allows you to earn compound interest on your investments which increases your returns.

Here are a few other reasons why investing is important and why you should consider starting early.

- **Wealth creation.** Everyone has their own idea of what wealth looks like. To some, it could mean having a certain amount of money in the bank, while others may define wealth as achieving certain financial goals they set for themselves. Whatever your definition may be, if you want to build wealth, investing your money can help you get there. You build wealth by investing in assets that have the potential to increase in value in the future. Whether your goal is to pay off debt, start a business, buy a home, or save for retirement, investing can help you achieve your goals.
- **Retirement.** To retire well, you need to have funds saved to live off of when you stop working. It's never too early to start planning for your retirement and making sure you have money to live off of for 20 or

258 | GEORGIA I. LAINIOTIS, MBA, MA

30 years. To start investing for retirement, determine when you want to retire and what kind of lifestyle you want to live. You can then create an investment strategy that aligns with your retirement goals.

- **To beat inflation.** Inflation is the increase in the price of goods and services. If prices of goods and services increase over time, this results in your money buying less today than it did yesterday. If there is inflation over a longer period of time, your money will continue to be worth less, and the cost of living will continue to get higher. One effective way to beat inflation is to invest your money. If your investments earn more than the inflation rate, it means your money will be worth more in the future than it is today.

- **To earn compound interest.** Investing gives you an opportunity to earn compound interest. Compound interest is the interest you earn on your invested funds calculated on both the capital and the accumulated interest from previous periods. It is also known as interest on interest.

Compound interest can help you grow wealth fast. For example, if you invested $200 per month for 15 years at a 5% interest rate, your total contribution over that period would be $36,000 and your interest would be $17,457.79 bringing your balance to $53,457.79. The easiest way to calculate compound interest on your investments is to use an online compound interest calculator such as the one you find on www.thebalancemoney.com.

HOW MUCH MONEY SHOULD YOU INVEST

When it comes to investing, there's no one size fits all strategy you can employ. We all have different goals, income opportunities, and financial obligations. To create an investment strategy, consider the timelines for your investment goals and the amount of risk you're willing to take.

Depending on what you intend to invest in, you don't need much to start investing these days. The key is to contribute more than your initial investment amount whenever you can so that you have more money to grow over time.

There are different investment strategies you can choose to build your portfolio, but before we get into those, let me emphasize the importance of seeking the help of a finance expert when making financial decisions. Seeking professional help will allow you to make informed decisions and save you from making mistakes and possibly suffering losses.

So, just how much of your income should you put aside toward building your investment portfolio? In Chapter 4, we learned about different types of budgeting systems you can use to allocate your after-tax income. The same strategies apply to investing. For example, you can use the 50/30/20 budget rule where you allocate 50% of your after-tax income toward your basic necessities, 30% to your wants, and 20% towards your savings and investments.

Set aside 20% of your net income for your savings and investments. You could contribute toward a mutual fund account, purchase a property for long-term holding, or invest in the stock market.

Before investing, have at least three months of emergency funds saved up for your living expenses in case of an unforeseen event such as loss of employment, or if you're faced with a health challenge and cannot work for a while.

Another strategy you can use for your investments is the four percent rule. The four percent rule is based on research conducted by financial advisor William Bengen back in 1994. Bengen used historical data on stock and bond returns dating back 50 years—from 1926 to 1976—to challenge the previous idea that living off five percent of your retirement savings yearly in retirement was a safe bet (Blankenship, 2023).

Bengen concluded that one could live off of a four percent withdrawal in the year they retire and adjust the amount for inflation each subsequent year for 30 years. To conduct his study, Bengen used a 60/40 portfolio model (60% equities, 40% bonds). To note, however, his research was done during a period of higher bond returns (higher interest rates) compared with the current rates.

While the four percent rule can help you determine how much you'll need to live comfortably after retirement, it doesn't take into account the different circumstances you may encounter in the future, such as the following.

- **Market fluctuations.** There's no economy that ever stays perfectly consistent for the entirety of your retirement years. Market conditions are ever-changing based on a nation's political, economic, and environmental factors. In a booming economy, withdrawing four percent or more annually might make sense; however, during times of uncertainty, you might need to cut back on your spending.
- **Medical expenses.** As you age, it's common to spend more on medical expenses, but it's difficult to predict what those expenses will be and how much you'll need to cover them. Another factor that the four percent rule does not take into account is life expectancy. The longer you live, the longer you'll need your savings to last.
- **Personal tax rate.** The four percent rule also does not consider your personal tax rate, which is affected by different factors such as the size of your investment accounts, other sources of income, credits, deductions, and the state you live in.

How Do You Use the Four Percent Rule to Invest in Your Future?

With the four percent rule, you work backward. You must first determine how much you'll need to live off of after retirement. You'll need to come up with an estimate of how much you expect to spend each year. To do this, consider the following expenses:

- rent or mortgage;
- the annual cost of groceries;
- the annual cost of medication and healthcare;
- transportation costs including car payments, maintenance, or public transportation; and,
- the amount you intend to spend on traveling.

You can add other expenses to the list based on your life-style. Once you've determined how much you'll need for your living expenses, take into account your discretionary expenses. Say you expect to spend $50,000 annually. Set aside an additional $5,000 as a cushion for unexpected expenses. This brings the total amount you'll live off of to $55,000.

If you expect to receive $20,000 annually from your Social Security benefits, then there's no need to withdraw the entire $55,000 from your retirement savings—you only need to withdraw $35,000 annually.

Once you figure out how much money you'll need to withdraw from your retirement savings each year, you can now use the four percent rule to come up with the total amount you'll need to save before you enter retirement. To do this, divide $35,000 by 0.04 to get $875,000. This means, $875,000 will last you 30 years if you only withdraw $35,000 (four percent) a year.

MAKING SMART INVESTMENT MOVES

It can be tempting to put off investing. You may think you're still young and have your whole life ahead of you. Or, you may be thinking that it's too complicated and you don't know where to begin. The good news is you don't need millions to start building your investment portfolio. With just a few hundred dollars you can put your money to work for you and watch it grow in the upcoming years. This is how you can do it.

Pick an Investment Strategy

Deciding on what investment strategy to start with depends on your savings goals and your timeframe.

For example, if your savings goal is a long-term one such as retirement, you can invest your money in stocks. Picking specific stocks can be a complicated process, which is why it's better to invest in stocks through low-cost stock mutual funds, index funds, or ETFs.

Suppose you're saving for a short-term goal and you need the money in less than five years. In that case, investing in stocks would be riskier—you're better off keeping your money in your savings account, cash management account, or low-risk investments such as short-term bond funds.

Understand Your Investment Options

Once you decide on your investment strategy you'll need to decide what to invest in. Before making the final decision on what to invest in, make sure that you understand each financial instrument you intend to invest in, the risk associated with it, and whether that risk is within your risk tolerance. Remember to seek advice from a financial expert before making any investment decisions.

The most popular investments for anyone starting to build their investment portfolio include:

- **Stocks.** In the short term, stocks can be extremely volatile. You need to plan to hold them for a longer period—say, three to five years.
- **Bonds.** If you're looking for a reliable stream of income, bonds are a better option, though they have lower gains than stocks.
- **Mutual funds.** Buying shares in the fund—which often has diversified investments—reduces your risk and potentially increases your returns.
- **Exchange-traded funds (ETFs).** Much like mutual funds, ETFs allow you to invest in stocks, bonds, or

other assets. ETFs have other benefits, as well, such as low management fees, which makes them cheaper to own than mutual funds.

Open an Investment Account

If you do not have an employer-sponsored retirement account like a 401(k), you can open an individual retirement account (IRA). It could either be a traditional or Roth IRA.

If you're investing for a goal other than for retirement you may want to avoid retirement accounts. They are designed to be used for retirement and have restrictions on when you can make withdrawals. Instead, consider a taxable brokerage account that allows you to withdraw funds at any time without additional taxes or penalties.

Decide How Much You Want to Invest

How much you should invest depends on your income, financial obligations, and investment goals, among other factors.

You can use the 50/30/20 rule and invest 20% of your income each month. You don't need tons of money to build your investment portfolio. Start small and work your way up to it over time.

Start Building Your Investment Portfolio Early

Investing while you're still young is one of the best ways to build a solid foundation for your finances. You get to compound your earnings, and over time your investment returns will earn their own return. If you're worried about the size of your contribution and whether it's enough, there are plenty of investments available for relatively small amounts, such as index funds, exchange-traded funds, and mutual funds. Invest an amount that feels manageable— given your financial situation. It doesn't matter whether you invest $10,000 a month or $1,000 a month. What matters is that you make regular contributions to your investment accounts.

Say you invest $500 every month for 10 years and earn a five percent average annual return. At the end of the 10-year period, your account balance will be $77,996.03.

$60,500 of that amount is money you'd have contributed (the $500 monthly contributions) and $17,496.03 is interest you'd earn on your investment over a 10-year period.

RETIREMENT PLANS

When you're in your teens and twenties, retirement seems like a long time away. Your priorities right now could be to finish school, buy a car, and travel the world. While it's great that you may have different priorities, there are several benefits to starting saving for retirement early. Most employers offer some type of retirement savings plan, which means you can start building your retirement fund as soon as you start earning a salary.

While you cannot predict the future, you can prepare for unexpected life events. Building a retirement fund early ensures that you are financially prepared for the years when you won't be able to work.

Benefits of Planning for Retirement Early

• **Compounding pays off.** Compound interest is one of the most significant benefits of saving for retirement early. It allows your invested funds to grow significantly due to interest building upon itself over time. Though the rate of return is not guaranteed, when you start saving for retirement earlier, you're likely to end up with more money in your account than if you wait until later in your career.

• **You can make aggressive investment decisions.** All investments come with a certain level of risk. The higher the potential rate of return from an investment, the more risk it carries. Building a retirement fund when you are young allows you to take more risks with your investments and still have time to recoup any losses you incur.

While riskier investments may result in higher potential returns, they can also have large fluctuations in value. Always consider your risk tolerance before making investment decisions.

• **You can have an early retirement.** If you want to retire before the age of 65, building a retirement fund early can allow you to take an early retirement. Once you pay off all your debt and have saved enough money to pay for your living expenses, you can retire early and spend more time fulfilling your other life goals such as traveling or doing philanthropic work and giving back to the community.

Planning for your retirement early can help you reach your retirement goal and allow you to pursue a new career or hobbies you may not have time for now. Focusing on your retirement savings in your early years can mean more flexibility and freedom in the future.

- **Take advantage of employer contributions.** If your employer offers 401(k) employer match—meaning they deposit money in your 401(k) account to match your contributions—ensure that you contribute enough to take full advantage of the match. For example, if you earn $75,000 per year and your employer offers to match 50% of your 401(k) contributions, up to five percent of your salary, your contribution would be $3,750 and your employer would contribute another $1,875.

This is free money you can take advantage of that can add up over your working life. And, if you contribute to a 401(k) with an employer match from the start of your career, you'll have a significant amount of money saved up by the time you retire.

- **Social security is not guaranteed.** Your Social Security benefits may not be enough to cover your living expenses during retirement. Have your own retirement savings and do not rely on your Social Security benefits only.

• **Tax benefits.** Your 401(k) earnings accrue on a tax-deferred basis; meaning, the dividends and capital gains that accumulate inside your 401(k) are not subject to tax until you start making withdrawals. So, opt for tax diversification. Put your money into tax-free, tax-deferred, and taxable accounts. By doing so, you can withdraw your retirement savings strategically from all your accounts based on your future circumstances.

• **Account for inflation.** While inflation is a reality we live with our entire lives, people who build a retirement fund earlier in their careers have a better chance of having their retirement savings keep up with the rate of inflation.

TYPES OF RETIREMENT PLANS

If you're wondering which investment plan you should choose to start saving for retirement, here are some common retirement plans you can choose from.

• **401(k).** The 401(k) is a popular investment vehicle for saving for retirement. It has great tax benefits for employees who contribute toward their 401(k) accounts with their salaries. If you get matching contributions from your employer, you'll have a significant amount of money by the time you retire.

With the 401(k) plan your employer manages your plan. They select the broker and investment options you can choose from, and you choose which investments you wish to contribute your money towards and how you can contribute.

• **Roth IRA.** A Roth IRA is a tax-advantaged individual retirement account to which you can contribute after-tax dollars. With the Roth IRA your earnings grow tax-free and you can withdraw your money tax-free after the age of 59½ (if the account has been active for not less than five years). In other words, since you pay taxes on your contributions to your Roth IRA, all future withdrawals will be tax-free.

• **SIMPLE IRA.** Employers (including self-employed individuals), can contribute toward SIMPLE IRAs if they have no more than 100 employees who earned at least $5,000 in the previous year. With a SIMPLE IRA you can have your contributions deducted from your paycheck and your money will grow tax-free until retirement.

• **Traditional IRA.** A traditional individual retirement account (IRA) is a retirement account that grows tax-deferred. This means your contributions are made from your paycheck before tax deductions. Your money will grow in that account tax-deferred and you'll only start paying taxes on your earnings and contributions once you start making withdrawals. This lowers your taxable income during the years you'll be making contributions but increases your taxable income in retirement.

For example, say you earn $70,000 annually and contribute 10% of your salary to a traditional 401(k). You'll get a $7,000 tax deduction. In your W-2 form (wage and tax statement), your total wages will appear as $63,000, since you contributed $7,000 to your traditional 401(k). This lowers your taxable income and your taxes. However, once you start withdrawing your money after retirement you'll be required to pay federal taxes and state taxes if applicable.

• **SEP IRA.** A simplified employee pension (SEP) is an individual retirement account (IRA) designed for employers or self-employed individuals. SEP IRA contributions are tax-deductible and contributions are considered employer contributions, so your employer makes them on your behalf.

A SEP IRA has similar features to an IRA. Your investment grows tax-deferred until retirement, when your distributions become taxable income. The SEP IRA may be a better investment option for people without an employer-sponsored plan.

• **Solo 401(k).** A solo 401(k) is a plan for business owners who have no employees. This plan allows you to save a large amount of money both from the business as the employer and out of your own paycheck as the employee.

A solo 401(k) has some benefits over other types of retirement accounts available to self-employed individuals. So, if you choose to be a freelancer or an independent contractor, you can still have a retirement savings plan and reap the tax benefits on your savings plan.

PROTECTING YOUR INVESTMENT FUND

Banking has evolved so much over the years. With advancements in technology and most banks taking a shift to digital banking, managing your finances has become secure and sophisticated at the same time. Fraud is on the rise and fraudsters are always looking for ways to scam people out of their hard-earned cash.

For this reason, you should always be on high alert and have fraud prevention measures in place to protect your assets. Building wealth takes time and hard work. You sacrifice instant gratification to build your savings and pursue your financial goals, which is why it's important to find ways to protect what you've achieved and take measures to avoid the growing number of financial scams out there.

Here are a few common scams and ways that can help you outsmart fraudsters so you can keep your assets protected.

Ransomware

Ransomware is malware that restricts your access files on your computer, smartphone, or tablet by encrypting them until you pay a ransom. Hackers often request a ransom ranging from a few hundred dollars to thousands payable in funds like Bitcoin in exchange for the decryption key (Fruhlinger, 2020).

Ransomware gains access to your devices when you click on attachments that you receive in your email or a link that leads to a contaminated file or website. Once opened and downloaded, they can take over your computer.

Ransomware can also affect a network of computers in the workplace or be passed around on a contaminated thumb drive.

How to Avoid Ransomware:

- Run antivirus software on your computer to search for and remove malware.
- Avoid clicking on attachments and links in emails or texts from untrusted sources.

Phishing

Phishing is an attack that attempts to steal your money or your identity. Phishing experts use emails or texts that look just like they're from banks, popular merchants, or someone you may know to get you to reveal your personal information such as credit card numbers, bank information, or passwords.

How to Avoid Phishing

- When you receive an email or text that looks suspicious, always do an online search to verify the website or phone number.
- You can also contact the merchant to confirm if the text or email is valid.

- Be wary of clicking on links or opening attachments on online platforms.

Debt Collection Fraud

Fraudsters sometimes pose as collectors and can contact you by phone, text messages, fax, mail, or email to try to get you to pay debts that you don't owe, or that you've settled already

How to Avoid Debt Collection Fraud

- Look out for red flags such as callers who don't provide written proof of the debt you supposedly owe.
- Ask the agent for their name, company details, business address, and professional debt collector license number.
- Check whether the collection agency is legitimate by doing an online search.
- Contact the debt collection agency to confirm if the debt collector is legitimate.
- Never give out your personal information until you've verified the debt.

Check Overpayment Scam

This scam is common in situations where you participate in a competition and you win a prize, but you're told to send money covering taxes and fees. Scammers send you a counterfeit check and ask you to pay them the excess between the intended amount and the amount on the check. Or, if you sell items online and the buyer (scammer) "mistakenly" over-pays and asks you to send back the extra amount.

How to Avoid Check Overpayment Scam

- If you're selling items online, don't accept checks for more than your selling price.
- Consider using a secure online payment service.

Employment Fraud

Fraudsters can pose as employers or human resource personnel offering employment opportunities, including working remote jobs. They offer too-good-to-be-true benefits such as easy work for high pay.

How to Avoid Employment Fraud

- If the job offer is from a well-known organization, visit their website to confirm if the job was posted there.
- Research a company's profile and legitimacy on websites such as LinkedIn.
- Avoid job offers that don't involve interviews.

Romance Fraud

Fraudsters use fake profiles on dating sites and social media to pretend to fall in love with you to win your trust, and then ask for money or your personal information. Scammers often request money for airline tickets, medical expenses, or temporary financial setbacks.

How to Avoid Romance Fraud

- Avoid sending money to people you don't know, even if they've professed their love to you.
- Avoid giving too much of your personal information to people you meet online.
- Always safeguard your banking details and personal information.

Online Shopping Scams

While online shopping is convenient for shoppers, it comes with its own risks. Online shopping scams take many forms, from fake online shops that sell items that never get delivered to those that deliver fake or substandard merchandise.

How to Avoid Online Shopping Scams

- Shop with reputable sellers on secure sites.
- Always check the URL security of a site you are shopping on and be on high alert for signs of fake

sites such as spelling errors and character replacement.

- Avoid offers that seem too good to be true.

Debit Card Scams

Debit card scams can happen fast and without you noticing, and they come in different forms.

- **Distraction theft.** Fraudsters can pose as authority figures or stand close to you to distract you while you're using an ATM to steal your debit card information.
- **Card skimming.** This is another common debit card scam where your card gets quickly swiped through a device that collects your debit card information. Your card details can also be skimmed at ATMs where there are hidden cameras.

How to Avoid Debit Card Scams

- Be aware of people trying to distract you when you're making debit card transactions.
- Keep an eye on your card when you hand it over to make a payment and cover your PIN when using an ATM.
- Constantly check your transaction history in your account.

The key to securing your financial future is having an investment strategy that will help you build your retirement savings fund. To choose an investment strategy that will align with your goals, consider how much you're earning, your financial obligations, and your financial goals.

Remember, every investment opportunity comes with some level of risk, so ensure that the risk you're taking matches your risk tolerance. Also, take the necessary measures to protect your investments. You don't want to lose your money to fraudsters after working so hard to build your savings.

We've learned quite a lot about how you can invest your money and let it work for you, but how do you protect yourself from unforeseen circumstances such as theft and loss of property? Next, we'll learn ways in which you can protect your assets so you can have peace of mind knowing that your financial future is secured.

10

INTRODUCTION TO SAFEGUARDING WITH INSURANCE

Insurance is like a guardian angel standing by your side during life's unexpected challenges.

— UNKNOWN

No one knows what the future holds. Unexpected life events such as illness, accidents, and even death can happen at any time—whether you're prepared to handle them or not. This is why it's important to protect yourself and your assets in case of the occurrence of any such unfortunate events.

WHAT IS INSURANCE?

Insurance is a legal contract represented by a policy in which the policyholder receives financial protection or reimbursement in case of an unfortunate event or a crisis, such as accidental injuries or damage to a vehicle or property.

To benefit from the insurance policy, the policyholder must pay a regular amount of money, known as a premium, to the insurance company. In short, a premium is the amount that you pay an insurance company to cover your risk.

When you have valuable possessions you cannot pay for if they are lost or damaged, taking an insurance policy out on them is the wisest thing you can do to protect your valuable possessions. It gives you peace of mind knowing that if something goes wrong, the insurance company will cover the loss and that there will be less impact on your finances.

Types of Insurance Available for College Students

Personal Liability Insurance

Accidents are unpredictable; anything can happen. For example, someone can injure themselves while attending a party you organized at your apartment. Personal liability insurance coverage can save you from paying legal fees and medical expenses out of your own pocket. This coverage covers injuries on your property and damages to other people's property. Personal liability insurance is usually included in your homeowner or renter's policy.

Health Insurance

When you live with your parents at home you can be added to your parent's health insurance plan until you turn 26. Your parents can add you to their plan in two ways.

- **Job-based plans.** Your parents can add you to their job-based insurance plan during the plan's yearly open enrollment period or during a special enrollment period.
- **Plans bought through the Health Insurance Marketplace®.** Your parents can add you to an existing Marketplace during the yearly open enrollment period or special enrollment period.

They can also add you when they apply for a new plan.

If you are going to study in another state and are still covered by your parents, they may need to contact their insurance provider to ensure there are in-network insurance providers close to your location. If there aren't in-network healthcare insurance providers close by, consider doing your routine medical check with your local practitioner while you're still living at home. But, you'll need to create a plan to handle emergency situations once you head off to college.

If you're 26 and above, you have the option to buy your own healthcare insurance coverage.

Here are five types of healthcare insurance coverage that you can access.

- **COBRA.** The Consolidated Omnibus Budget Reconciliation Act of 1985 (COBRA) is designed to protect people from losing their health insurance. It allows you to continue benefiting from your health insurance coverage when you lose your job or have reduced work hours.
- **Your parents' plan.** In the United States, you can stay on your parent's health insurance plan until the age of 26.
- **Medicaid.** Medicaid, also known as medical assistance, is a government-funded health

insurance that's available only to low-income earners and people with disabilities. Check your state's Department of Health and Human Development (HHD) program to see if you're eligible.

- **Individual policy.** Individual health policy covers your health and medical care. Take into consideration that buying health insurance on your own can be a more costly option than sharing risk with a group of people; for example, other students or colleagues. You may have to pay more premiums if you're considered a higher risk; for example, if you engage in activities that affect your health, such as smoking.

- **Employer plans.** This is usually the least expensive option since employers often help pay for part of the insurance. Some companies offer health insurance coverage to employees on their first day of work, while others will make you work for a period of between 30 to 90 days.

- **Short-term policy.** Most insurance companies sell short-term or student insurance policies to bridge the gap between school and your first job.

- **Subsidized state program.** If you're under 19, uninsured, and your family's income is below a certain level, you might qualify for the State Children's Health Insurance Program (SCHIP). Benefits differ in each state, so ensure that you check with your state's Department of Health and Human Services.

Auto Insurance Coverage

One of the first things that you'll need to do when you start driving is to get auto insurance. If you drive your own car, you must have your own insurance policy, and if you're driving your parent's car, you'll need to be an insured driver under their policy. In that case your parent or guardian needs to add your name to his or her policy as a licensed, insured driver of that vehicle.

Requirements for Auto Insurance

All 50 states in the U.S., except for New Hampshire, require drivers to have at least a specified minimum amount of liability insurance. Liability insurance covers drivers who are found to be at fault in a car accident. It comes in two basic types:

- Bodily injury liability (BI) coverage.
- Property damage liability (PD) coverage.

Bodily injury liability insurance pays for medical and other expenses if you injure someone in a car accident in which you're considered to be at fault.

Property damage liability coverage is required by law in most states. It covers the cost of car repairs if you are at fault in a car accident that damages someone's vehicle or property, but it does not usually cover damage to your car.

Other states may also require that you purchase comprehensive, collision, underinsured or uninsured motorist, or personal injury protection (PIP) coverage.

If you finance your vehicle through an auto loan, your creditor may require that you purchase collision and comprehensive coverage and maintain it until your loan is paid off. Collision insurance covers damages to your vehicle from an accident and comprehensive insurance covers your car against fire, theft, damages to the windshield, and glass repairs.

Other types of car insurance are optional, but if you want to make your insurance coverage as comprehensive as possible, you might consider adding them.

These include:

- roadside assistance insurance;
- medical payments coverage, or MedPay;
- towing and labor coverage; and,
- rental reimbursement coverage.

How to Save on Car Insurance

Practicing road safety can help minimize your odds of getting involved in an accident and can also keep your car insurance rates as low as possible.

Here are a few other ways you save on insurance.

- Enroll in automatic bill payment and electronic document delivery if it qualifies you for discounts.
- Find out if your insurance company offers student discounts.
- Consider bundling your car and renter's policies with another insurer to lower your premiums.
- Raise the deductibles on your policy—if you can afford to pay them out of pocket.
- Check if there are discounts for taking driver's education or defensive driving courses.

Renter's Insurance

If you plan to live off campus, consider renter's insurance. It's an affordable way to protect your belongings. Renter's insurance covers possessions inside your rental property from theft or damage.

If you live on campus, you can cover your belongings with homeowner's insurance. Take stock of what you bring to campus—preferably with photos—and keep all your receipts in case anything is damaged or stolen from your room. You can also protect your expensive electronics such as laptops, tablets, and cell phones from electrical faults with residential equipment breakdown insurance.

Gap Insurance Coverage

Gap insurance covers your vehicle in the event of car theft or an accident where your car is totaled. It pays the difference between what your insurance company pays for the total loss or theft and the balance you owe on the car.

For example, if your auto loan balance is $35,000 and based on depreciation your vehicle is now worth $30,000. If you're involved in an accident or your vehicle is stolen, your auto insurance policy will cover the $30,000, because that is what your car is worth. Meaning, you'd still be responsible for paying off the $35,000 loan balance. And, if your insurance company reimburses $30,000, you'd still owe your creditor another $5,000. With gap insurance, the $5,000 difference would be covered as well.

Is Gap Insurance a Legal Requirement?

If you finance or rent out a new car, you may need gap insurance, but there are no state or federal laws that require you to take it out. When you finance a vehicle, your creditor maintains ownership until your loan is fully paid off. If your car is stolen, damaged, or totaled before you pay off the loan, your creditor loses money. To avoid that risk, creditors often require borrowers to purchase specific types of coverage, including comprehensive and collision coverage. Some creditors may also require that you take out gap insurance.

Who Needs Gap Insurance?

You need gap coverage if you:

- rent out your vehicle;
- finance your new vehicle for more than 60 months;
- purchase a vehicle with less than a 20% down payment; or,
- purchase a vehicle that will quickly depreciate, for example, some luxury or sports cars.

Whether or not you should take out gap insurance depends on the value of your car and how much you owe on your auto loan. If your vehicle depreciates and dips below your loan balance, you may want to consider buying gap insurance.

How and Where to Get Gap Insurance

Most dealerships sell gap insurance, making it easy to buy coverage when you buy a car. Some banks and credit unions also sell gap insurance.

In most states, insurers will automatically add gap coverage when you purchase a new vehicle. So, check with your insurance agent to see if you're already covered.

Advantages of Gap Insurance

- When you buy gap insurance from your primary auto insurance company you'll only need to file a single claim if your car is stolen or damaged.
- It reduces the financial burden when you're involved in an accident.
- It allows you to buy an expensive vehicle with less worry.
- The annual cost is relatively low, often between $200 to $500 (RIVELLI, n.d.).

OTHER TYPES OF INSURANCE

Pet Insurance

Like other policies, you also pay a monthly premium to your insurer to be covered with pet insurance. If your pet falls sick or is injured, you'll pay the veterinarian up front and submit a claim to the insurance agency for reimbursement. Most pet health insurance plans do not pay the vet directly, but reimburse you, instead.

Pet insurance reduces the financial burden of unexpected veterinary costs. With the right coverage plan, you can have peace of mind and get the best health care for your pet.

What Does Pet Insurance Cover?

Though pet insurance may not cover every condition your pet has, the best pet insurance plans often cover the most expensive health treatment. When taking out pet insurance coverage, find a plan that covers:

- medication;
- Surgery (for example, cruciate ligament tears or cataracts);
- unexpected injuries or accidents;
- illnesses such as cancer, hip dysplasia, parvovirus, and glaucoma;
- X-rays, blood tests, MRIs, and other tests; and,
- emergency examination fees.

Benefits of Pet Insurance

- It ensures great healthcare for your pet. Depending on the policy you choose, pet insurance covers a wide range of treatments for parasite-borne diseases, cataracts, dental issues, fractures, pregnancy complications, and so on.
- Pet insurance is also beneficial for pets that may need additional healthcare as they age.
- It keeps you from dipping into your savings. Just like humans, pets can also go through major illnesses, and the cost of treatment can be very expensive.

- It saves you money on hospitalization and expensive medical treatments.

Life Insurance

Life insurance is a contract between a policyholder and an insurance company where the insurance company promises to pay a sum of money—referred to as a death benefit—upon the death of the policyholder, in exchange for a premium. Life insurance protects the future of your loved ones by paying out a lump sum amount if an unfortunate event such as death occurs.

There are two types of life insurance.

1. **Term life insurance.** Term life insurance provides coverage for a certain amount of time and the premium payments stay the same amount for the duration of the policy.
2. **Permanent life insurance.** Permanent life insurance is a lifelong policy that usually builds cash value. The policy allows you to borrow against its cash value or make withdrawals. In other words, you could say it's the savings portion of the policy.

Some life insurance policies provide you with a maturity benefit when your policy reaches its term.

Benefits of Having Life Insurance

Life insurance offers several benefits to you and your loved ones.

- **Financial Security.** The proceeds from life insurance can be used by your family as an income replacement to pay for living expenses.
- **Wealth Creation.** Some life insurance plans offer you the option to invest and grow your money. This prepares you financially for your future needs.
- **Tax Benefits.** In the event of death—if it's within your policy term—your beneficiaries can make a claim and receive the death benefit, tax-free.
- **Disability Insurance.** Disability insurance pays out a portion of your income if you cannot work and earn a living because of an injury or disability. You can get coverage through your employer, the government, or private insurers. There are two types of disability insurance policies.
- **Short-term disability insurance.** This policy provides immediate protection after an incident and a maximum benefit period of two years.
- **Long-term disability insurance.** This lasts for two years. Some policies provide financial protection up until retirement.

Disability insurance can supplement your income if you're unable to work due to injury or sudden illness. It can help you pay for your day-to-day expenses, relieve you from the stress caused by the inability to work, and to provide for yourself. In the U.S., you can also access two types of federal disability programs under the Social Security Administration (SSA).

- **Social Security Disability Insurance (SSDI).** This plan pays monthly benefits to employees who are unable to work due to an illness or impairment that can last up to a year or result in death. The SSDI is designed for people who have worked in jobs covered by Social Security.
- **Supplemental Security Income (SSI).** The SSI plan provides financial protection for people who are 65 years old or older with disabilities, and have little to no income and resources.

The eligibility requirements for federal disability programs include having a disability:

- that can last for at least 12 months or could result in death; and,
- that prevents you from doing any type of significant work.

EARLY BIRD ADVANTAGES

When you're young and vibrant, investing in health insurance may seem unnecessary, but investing in your health is as important as any other investment. When you're insured, you have peace of mind knowing that your future is secured. So, if you're wondering if you should get life insurance at the age of 20, here are a few reasons why you should consider it.

• **Secures your finances.** Buying an insurance policy earlier in life will prove to be beneficial in the future. For example, buying health insurance can help you secure your finances well in advance for medical emergencies. It prepares you for all kinds of emergencies, no matter how big they are.

• **You can easily pass the waiting period.** Most health insurance plans have a waiting period and other conditions before you can be fully covered by the plan. The waiting period can range from a few months to years, and you cannot make a claim during this period—even if an emergency arises. Buying an insurance policy earlier in life can help you easily pass the waiting period without worrying about emergencies.

• **Lowers chances of getting rejected.** Insurance companies have the right to reject an application if the risk of covering an individual is high, based on the age of the applicant and other factors. Applying for insurance while you're young reduces the chances of your application getting rejected.

• **Lower rates.** Buying insurance when you are young allows you to pay lower premiums on your insurance policy and your premiums remain the same for the duration of your policy—unless you change the amount of coverage.

For example, a health insurance policy covers ailments such as diabetes, heart disease, kidney failure, cancer, and so on. These health conditions often affect people later on in life. So, when you buy a health insurance policy in your twenties, the financial risk associated with your health is far less.

• **Renewability.** Renewability is important because, typically, you'd want to renew your insurance policy at the end of its term—that is, if your life circumstances don't change (for example, your health deteriorates and you're considered uninsurable). Renewability enables you to keep your current coverage—though you're likely to pay a higher premium.

Knowing that your most-prized possessions, including your health, are protected gives you peace of mind. When you work hard to secure your financial future for yourself, you want to rest assured that you'll enjoy the fruits of your hard labor later on in life.

For this reason, invest in insurance policies earlier in life and protect your valuable possessions and health. It may seem like an added expense in the short term, but the benefits will be worth it in the long run, and you'll ensure that your future family is well taken care of.

A Small Step You Can Take Right Now!

As I said, small steps can lead to massive results... and this is where one small step from you can make a massive difference.

Simply by sharing your honest opinion of this book, you'll show other young people where they can find all the financial knowledge they need to ensure a successful future.

Now how's that for a big result?! Thank you so much for your support.

Scan the QR code to leave a review!

CONCLUSION

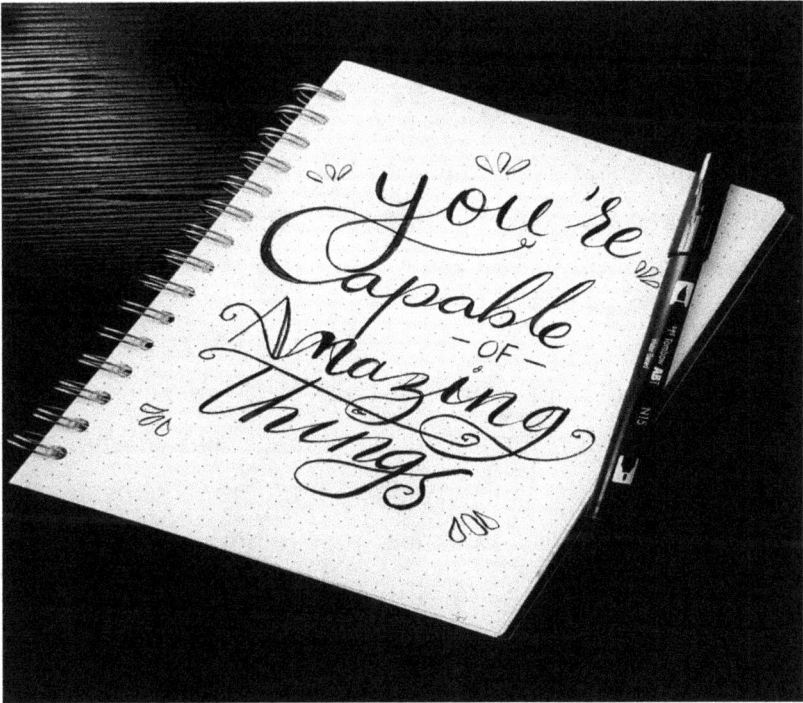

Procrastination is a silent killer of dreams. It delays you from taking action and can rob you of a bright future. We all have dreams, goals, and aspirations. Each of us has a vision of what we want the future to look like. It takes having a plan to turn that vision into reality. So, when you start procrastinating, ask yourself, "Where do I want to be five to ten years from now?"

Throughout this book, you've learned many tools to help you secure your financial future, with your mind being the most powerful of them all. You can use your mind to excel academically and in every other aspect of your life. Therefore, you must develop a positive attitude toward life and your finances and ensure you are educating yourself on financial best practices.

There will be times when you go through difficulties financially. You'll make investment mistakes as a new investor, for example, and that's okay. Understand that to learn and be a master of any craft, you must make mistakes. Embrace the lessons and move on.

Also, be mindful of your self-talk. Negative self-talk will only make you feel terrible about yourself and will not help you build the life you envision. Temporary setbacks are inevitable, but always remember they're not permanent. You can get yourself out of any situation if you're optimistic and willing to keep working toward achieving your goals.

To achieve your financial goals, be clear about what you're working toward and set a timeline for achieving them. This will help decide where to invest your money and for how long. Remember, before making any investment decisions, seek financial advice from a financial expert. Investments come with some level of risk and it's important to speak to someone trained to handle financial matters to help you make well-informed decisions.

Once you decide on your investment vehicles, start small. Nowadays, you don't need much to start investing. So, do not wait until you have tons of money; start with what you have and build your investment portfolio as you go. For example, start by using the 50/30/20 rule and invest 20% of your after-tax income. You can increase the percentage with time—when you start earning more income.

There are plenty of ways you can increase your income. You have talents that you may not have explored in the past. Now is the time to use your natural gifts and talents and turn them into profit. In Chapter 2, we discussed different ways in which you can earn money while in school. Whether you choose to get an internship or be a freelancer, creating multiple income streams can help you earn more and puts you in a position to invest more of your money into income-generating assets. And when you start earning, remember to honor your tax obligation. Paying state and federal taxes is not only the right thing to do but it also saves you money.

Building wealth takes time and discipline. It does not end with investing money and watching it grow over time, but it requires you to cultivate healthy spending habits as well. Delay instant gratification and you'll avoid The Diderot Effect. Always keep the end goal in mind. This does not mean depriving yourself of the simple pleasures of life, but it means setting a spending limit for yourself and sticking to it.

Keep in mind that a budget can help you achieve your financial goals. It allows you to put your money to work so you can account for every dollar you make. So, be sure to download budgeting software or create a budget worksheet to keep track of your spending.

Now, perhaps you're thinking, "I want to fund my education, but don't have enough money saved up for college. Should I still invest my income, or should I save for college first?" Well, the answer lies in identifying your goals and determining your risk appetite. You can put your money into a long-term investment vehicle like stocks and still manage to pay for your education by applying for student loans and scholarships. This way you get to build your credit score, which will be beneficial in the future when you want to apply for a bigger loan for larger purchases such as putting down a deposit for a home. But, remember that debt, if not managed, can ruin your credit score, which can make it difficult for you to access credit from borrowers.

A college savings account is another way you can start saving for college. Open a 529 plan and make contributions to it, and watch your money grow tax-free over time.

Finally, having your money work for you is only part of building wealth. The other part is to ensure that your assets are protected. Purchasing an insurance policy is the best thing you can do for your financial future. For example, health insurance ensures that you receive the best health care when you finally need it without dipping into your savings. And, life insurance ensures that your loved ones are taken care of in the unfortunate event of your death. Each type of insurance we discussed in Chapter 10 has benefits and is designed to help you get through emergencies without financial strain.

Before I close off, let me say, I applaud you for taking the time to read this book till the end. I hope that the tools outlined in this book will help you start your financial journey, and that as you keep implementing the ideas I've shared you'll build a solid foundation for your finances. Remember, small steps can lead to massive results. It's not just the size of your investment that matters, but how consistent you are in following your financial plan.

Paul Getty (n.d.) once said, "Men of means look at making money as a game which they love to play." So, go play and enjoy your journey to financial freedom!

REFERENCES

11 Benefits of Having An Abundance Mindset - Eleven Recruiting - IT Recruiting, IT Staffing and IT Jobs. (2022, February 17). Eleven Recruiting. https://elevenrecruit ing.com/benefits-of-having-an-abundance-mindset/

11 Ways to Stick to Your Budget. (n.d.). Valleyfirst. Retrieved May 17, 2023, from https://www.valleyfirst.com/simple-advice/money/ways-to-stick-to-your-budget

56 Easy Ways For Teens To Make Money Fast in 2023 - No Experience Required. (2022, October 28). Scholaroo. https://scholaroo.com/blog/ways-for-teens-to-make-money/

A quote from Song of a Nature Lover. (n.d.). Goodreads. Retrieved April 26, 2023, from https://www.goodreads.com/quotes/10896631-create-from-the-heart-for-nature-rewards-a-person-not

Acko, T. (2021, June 9). *8 Benefits of Buying Health Insurance at a Young Age.* Acko General Insurance. https://www.acko.com/articles/health-insurance/8-benefits-of-buying-health-insurance-at-a-young-age/

Adams, S. (2018, July 30). *The 10 Best Websites For Finding An Internship.* Forbes. https://www.forbes.com/sites/susanadams/2015/01/30/the-10-best-websites-for-finding-an-internship/?sh=3aa620a81b44

Agrawal, S. (2020, May 24). *Education Is the Most Powerful Weapon You Can Use To Change the World.* Thrive Global. https://community.thriveglobal.com/educa tion-is-the-most-powerful-weapon-you-can-use-to-change-the-world/

Alexander E.M. Hess. (2014, January 4). *Seven ways Americans pay taxes.* USA TODAY; USATODAY. https://www.usatoday.com/story/money/personalfi nance/2014/01/04/taxes-americans-pay/4307825/

Amadeo, K. (2022, January 29). *Interest Rates and How They Work.* The Balance. https://www.thebalancemoney.com/what-are-interest-rates-and-how-do-they-work-3305855

Amazing Benefits Of Buying Bulk Foods. (n.d.). The Source Bulk Foods UK. Retrieved May 29, 2023, from https://thesourcebulkfoods.co.uk/blogs/zero-waste/benefits-of-buying-bulk-foods

Anderson, M. (2011). *Advantages & Disadvantages of Working While Going to*

School. The Classroom. https://www.theclassroom.com/advantages-disadvan tages-of-working-while-going-to-school-12537639.html

Arslan, A. (2021, October 18). *The 10 Best Websites to Find an Internship. MUO.* https://www.makeuseof.com/best-websites-find-internship/

Ascensus. (n.d.). *529 Plans. Ascensus LLC.* Retrieved June 15, 2023, from https://www.ascensus.com/solutions/education/529-plans/

Bachman, S. (2017a). *The Benefits of Starting Your Career Early. Isu.edu.* https://blog.cetrain.isu.edu/blog/benefits-of-starting-your-career-early

Bachman, S. (2017b). *The Benefits of Starting Your Career Early. Isu.edu.* https://blog.cetrain.isu.edu/blog/benefits-of-starting-your-career-early

Baggerly, A. (2021a, December 4). *55 Easy Ways For Teens To Make Money In 2022. Inspired Budget.* https://inspiredbudget.com/55-ways-for-teens-to-make-money/

Baggerly, A. (2021b, December 5). *51 Budget Quotes To Keep You Motivated in 2022. Inspired Budget.* https://inspiredbudget.com/best-budget-quotes/

Bakke, D. (2019). *The Top 17 Investing Quotes of All Time. Investopedia.* https://www.investopedia.com/financial-edge/0511/the-top-17-investing-quotes-of-all-time.aspx

Bank of America. (2019). *Creating a Budget with a Personal Budget Spreadsheet. Better Money Habits.* https://bettermoneyhabits.bankofamerica.com/en/saving-budgeting/creating-a-budget

Banton, C. (2023, March 28). *Interest Rate. Investopedia.* https://www.investopedia.com/terms/i/interestrate.asp

Becker, J. (2015, August 12). *Understanding the Diderot Effect (and How To Overcome It). Becoming Minimalist.* https://www.becomingminimalist.com/diderot/

Beers, B. (2019). *Internet Banks: Pros and Cons. Investopedia.* https://www.investopedia.com/articles/pf/11/benefits-and-drawbacks-of-internet-banks.asp

Bell, A. (2019). *Understanding Your 401(k) and Its Benefits. Investopedia.* https://www.investopedia.com/articles/investing/102216/understanding-401ks-and-all-their-benefits.asp

Bell, A. (2020, January 28). *6 Reasons Why You NEED a Budget. Investopedia.* https://www.investopedia.com/financial-edge/1109/6-reasons-why-you-need-a-budget.aspx

Bennett, K. (2022, December 13). *Emergency Fund: What It Is And How To Start One. Bankrate.* https://www.bankrate.com/banking/savings/starting-an-emergency-fund/#how-much

Bennett, R. (2023, April 28). *How To Write A Check: A Step-By-Step Guide.* Bankrate. https://www.bankrate.com/banking/checking/how-to-write-a-check/#memo

Berry-Johnson, J. (2022, February 11). *Tax Prep Checklist: Everything You Need to File Your Taxes.* Forbes Advisor. https://www.forbes.com/advisor/taxes/tax-prep-checklist/

Blankenship, J. (2023, May 25). *What Is The 4% Rule For Retirement Withdrawals?* Bankrate. https://www.bankrate.com/retirement/what-is-the-4-percent-rule/

Brennan, C. (2017, May 31). *What are the best credit cards for teens?* Credit Karma. https://www.creditkarma.com/credit-cards/i/credit-cards-for-teens

Budgeting. (n.d.). *Practical Business Skills.* Retrieved May 17, 2023, from https://www.practicalbusinessskills.com/getting-started/financial-basics/budgeting

Burnette, M. (2023, February 17). *Emergency Fund: What it Is and Why it Matters.* NerdWallet. https://www.nerdwallet.com/article/banking/emergency-fund-why-it-matters

Burnette, margarette. (2021, April 23). *Is Online Banking Safe? How to Boost Your Banking Security.* NerdWallet. https://www.nerdwallet.com/article/banking/online-banking-security

BusyKid. (n.d.). *App Features | Busy Kid. BusyKid.* Retrieved May 25, 2023, from https://busykid.com/busykid-features/

By. (2022, April 17). *Sinking Fund vs Emergency Fund: What's the Difference? - Experian.* Experian. https://www.experian.com/blogs/ask-experian/sinking-fund-vs-emergency-fund/

Capital One. (2021, June 22). *8 Benefits of Having a Good Credit Score. Capital One.* https://www.capitalone.com/learn-grow/money-management/benefits-of-high-credit-score/

Carlos, A. (2022, April 28). *6 Reasons Why You Should Start Retirement Planning Early - District Capital.* District Capital Management. https://districtcapitalmanagement.com/start-retirement-planning-early/

Case, I. (2022, February 7). *Why Teenagers Should File a Tax Return — Even If It's Not Required by the IRS.* Money. https://money.com/teen-file-tax-return/

Cecillia Barr. (2012). *Types of Student Loans: Federal & Private Loan Options.* Debt.org. https://www.debt.org/students/types-of-loans/

CFI. (2019, November 12). *Types of Interest. Corporate Finance Institute.* https://corporatefinanceinstitute.com/resources/commercial-lending/types-of-interest/

CFNC. (2022, July 15). 10 Saving for College Tips for Parents (And What to Avoid) | CFNC. CNFC. https://www.cfnc.org/news/saving-for-college-tips/

Charity, S. D. (2019, July 17). Hidden in plain sight: Ending the overdraft debt trap. StepChange Debt Charity. https://medium.com/stepchange/hidden-in-plain-sight-ending-the-overdraft-debt-trap-120435ec2ae8

Chelsea. (2018, October 10). Understanding & Improving Your Money Mindset. Smart Money Mamas. https://smartmoneymamas.com/understanding-improving-your-money-mindset/

Chen, J. (n.d.). U.S. Savings Bonds. Investopedia. Retrieved June 15, 2023, from https://www.investopedia.com/terms/u/ussavingsbonds.asp

Chen, J. (2022, April 4). Owning Property Via a Real Estate Investment Trust. Investopedia. https://www.investopedia.com/terms/r/reit.asp

Choi, B. (n.d.). How to Manage Your Personal Cash Flow - NerdWallet. NerdWallet Canada. Retrieved May 23, 2023, from https://www.nerdwallet.com/ca/personal-finance/what-is-cash-flow

Clear, J. (2015, October 6). The Diderot Effect: Why We Want Things We Don't Need. James Clear. https://jamesclear.com/diderot-effect

cleartax. (n.d.). Investment - Definition, Understanding, and Why Investment is Important? Cleartax.in. Retrieved June 19, 2023, from https://cleartax.in/g/terms/investment

Code Cutters News. (n.d.). How to Get an Amazon Prime Video Free Trial. Cord Cutters News. Retrieved May 29, 2023, from https://cordcuttersnews.com/amazon-prime-video-free-trial/

College Choice. (2015, March 10). What Are the Major Expenses for Students? CollegeChoice. https://www.collegechoice.net/college-life/major-expenses-for-students/

Consumer Financial Protection Bureau. (n.d.). An essential guide to building an emergency fund. Consumer Financial Protection Bureau. Retrieved May 23, 2023, from https://www.consumerfinance.gov/an-essential-guide-to-building-an-emergency-fund/

consumerfinance.gov. (n.d.). Bill calendar. In consumerfinance.gov. consumerfinance.gov. Retrieved May 25, 2023, from https://files.consumerfinance.gov/f/documents/cfpb_ymyg_disabilities_bill-calendar.pdf

Costa, M. (2022, December 5). 18 Sinking Fund Categories To Consider In Your Budget. Clever Girl Finance. https://www.clevergirlfinance.com/sinking-fund-categories/

Council, Y. E. (2020, February 20). Council Post: Five Benefits Of Having Multiple Sources Of Income As An Entrepreneur. Forbes. https://www.forbes.com/sites/theyec/2020/02/25/five-benefits-of-having-multiple-sources-of-income-as-an-entrepreneur/?sh=6b94c31743bb

Credit Karma. (n.d.). Deserve® EDU Mastercard Reviews 2023. Credit Karma. Retrieved May 27, 2023, from https://www.creditkarma.com/reviews/credit-card/single/id/CCDeserve01

Crimson. (2023, March 17). Public vs Private Colleges: What's The Difference? - Crimson Education ZA. Crimson Education. https://www.crimsoneducation.org/za/blog/public-vs-private-colleges/

Cruz, R. (2022, October 4). How to Change Your Money Mindset. Ramsey Solutions. https://www.ramseysolutions.com/budgeting/understanding-your-money-mindset

Cruze, R. (2022, July 18). How to Change Your Spending Habits. Ramsey Solutions. https://www.ramseysolutions.com/budgeting/money-habits-we-need-to-break

Cruze, R. C. (2022, May 13). What Is a Sinking Fund and How Do You Create One? Ramsey Solutions. https://www.ramseysolutions.com/saving/stop-the-panic-sinking-fund

Dantus –, C.-R. (2019, April 2). Bill Calendar: Know what you owe and when it's due. Consumer Financial Protection Bureau. https://www.consumerfinance.gov/about-us/blog/budget-help-manage-your-monthly-expenses-bill-calendar/

Debt.org. (n.d.). Small Business Administration – What is SBA? History, Role & Programs. Debt.org. Retrieved June 4, 2023, from https://www.debt.org/small-business/sba/

DeMatteo, M. (2020, June 30). 10 questions to ask before you take out a personal loan. CNBC. https://www.cnbc.com/select/questions-before-taking-out-personal-loan/

Dinich, M. (2022, October 22). The 11 Types Of Personal Budget You Need To Know And Try | Wealth of Geeks. Wealth of Geeks. https://wealthofgeeks.com/types-of-personal-budget/

Doyle, A. (2021, August 19). Great Tips for Getting Your First Part-Time Job. The Balance. https://www.thebalancemoney.com/tips-for-getting-your-first-part-time-job-2058650

Earl, J. (2023, January 26). 3 benefits of filing your taxes early. Cbsnews. https://www.cbsnews.com/news/benefits-of-filing-taxes-early/

Elearnmarkets. (2016, January 27). Bank Account - 5 Simple Steps For Opening A

Bank Account. Elearnmarkets. https://blog.elearnmarkets.com/how-to-open-a-bank-account/

elearnmarkets. (2016, February 4). 9 Steps To Withdraw Money From ATM Machine. Elearnmarkets. https://blog.elearnmarkets.com/how-to-withdraw-money-from-atm-machine/

Equifax. (n.d.). How Are Credit Scores Calculated? | Equifax®. Equifax. Retrieved May 1, 2023, from https://www.equifax.com/personal/education/credit/score/how-is-credit-score-calculated/

FamZoo. (n.d.). FamZoo Prepaid Card FAQs. FamZoo. Retrieved May 25, 2023, from https://blog.famzoo.com/p/famzoo-card-faqs.html#cardholder-reqs

Farley, A. (2022, April 11). Why Should I Consider Investing? Investopedia. https://www.investopedia.com/ask/answers/why-should-i-invest/

Farm Bureau Financial Services. (2022, July 18). 6 Types of Insurance for College Students | Farm Bureau Financial Services. Farm Bureau Financial Services. https://www.fbfs.com/learning-center/what-to-ask-your-insurance-agent-before-your-kid-goes-to-college

Fay, B. (2012). Good Debt vs. Bad Debt - Types of Good and Bad Debts. Debt.org. https://www.debt.org/advice/good-vs-bad/

Fay, B. (2022, May 12). Types of Taxes – Income, Property, Goods, Services, Federal, State. Debt.org. https://www.debt.org/tax/type/

Federal Student Aid. (n.d.). Consolidating Student Loans. Federal Student Aid. Retrieved June 17, 2023, from https://studentaid.gov/manage-loans/consolidation#eligibility

Financial Gym. (2023, January 6). 4 Ways to Change Your Money Mindset from Scarcity to Abundance. The Financial Gym - as Seen on the TODAY Show. https://financialgym.com/blog/2020/12/17/4-ways-to-change-your-money-mindset-from-scarcity-to-abundance

First United Bank & Trust. (2021, July 20). The Advantages of Personal Internet Banking. First United Bank & Trust. https://mybank.com/the-advantages-of-personal-internet-banking/

Fontinelle, A. (n.d.). Overdraft Protection: Pros and Cons. Investopedia. Retrieved June 10, 2023, from https://www.investopedia.com/ask/answers/071114/what-are-pros-and-cons-overdraft-protection.asp

Fruhlinger, J. (2020, June 19). What is ransomware? How these attacks work & how to recover from them. CSO Online. https://www.csoonline.com/article/3236183/what-is-ransomware-how-it-works-and-how-to-remove-it.html

Getty, J. P. (n.d.). *J. Paul Getty Quote*. *A-Z Quotes*. Retrieved June 27, 2023, from https://www.azquotes.com/quote/818562

GoHenry. (n.d.-a). *privacy policy & cookies*. *Gohenry*. Retrieved May 29, 2023, from https://www.gohenry.com/uk/terms-and-conditions/privacy-policy/

GoHenry. (n.d.-b). *Smart Debit Cards for Kids*. *GoHenry*. Retrieved May 29, 2023, from https://www.gohenry.com/us/kids-debit-card/

Golden Haven. (2023, January 18). *Importance of Having Multiple Streams of Income | Golden Haven*. *Golden Haven Memorial Parks*. https://www.golden haven.com.ph/blog/importance-of-having-multiple-streams-of-income/

Goleman, D. (n.d.). *A quote from Emotional Intelligence*. *Goodreads*. Retrieved July 24, 2023, from https://www.goodreads.com/quotes/9567927-if-your-emotional-abilities-aren-t-in-hand-if-you-don-t

Gordon, W. (2013, August 31). *Top 10 Tricks to Get Discounts on Almost Anything*. *Lifehacker*. https://lifehacker.com/top-10-tricks-to-get-discounts-on-almost-anything-1227564502

Gorton, D. (2021, October 14). *Taxes*. *Investopedia*. https://www.investopedia.com/terms/t/taxes.asp

Group, T. C. (2022, August 15). *6 Reasons to Start Saving and Investing for Retirement Early*. *The Capital Group* . https://www.capgroupfinancial.com/insights/6-reasons-to-start-saving-and-investing-for-retirement-early

Haag, M. (2019, June 20). *17 Benefits of Working as a Teenager*. *LinkedIn*. https://www.linkedin.com/pulse/17-benefits-working-teenager-matt-haag/

Haan, K., & Main, K. (n.d.). *Indeed vs. Monster Comparison – Forbes Advisor*. *Www.forbes.com*. Retrieved June 11, 2023, from https://www.forbes.com/advisor/business/software/indeed-vs-monster/

Haegele, B. (2023, January 13). *7 Strategies for Managing Subscriptions in 2023 To Save Money*. *GOBankingRates*. https://www.gobankingrates.com/saving-money/savings-advice/managing-subscriptions-strategies-to-save-money/

Hakeenah, N. (2021, October 5). *Money Mindset: How An Abundance Mindset Can Make You Wealthy*. *Money254*. https://www.money254.co.ke/post/money-mind set-how-an-abundance-mindset-can-make-you-wealthy

Hall-Geisler, K., & Lobb, J. (2022, March 9). *What Is Gap Insurance for a Car? US News*. https://www.usnews.com/insurance/auto/gap-insurance

Hamm, T. (2019). *Here's When Buying in Bulk is Really Worth It*. *US News & World Report; U.S. News & World Report*. https://money.usnews.com/money/blogs/my-money/articles/when-buying-in-bulk-is-really-worth-it

HDFC Bank. (2013). 7 Tips for Safe Internet Banking | HDFC Bank. Hdfcbank.com. https://www.hdfcbank.com/personal/resources/learning-centre/secure/7-tips-for-safe-secure-internet-banking

Healy, W. (2016, August 4). How To Make a Budget: A Step-by-Step Guide. GOBankingRates. https://www.gobankingrates.com/saving-money/budgeting/budgeting-guide/

Helhoski, A., & Branch, T. (n.d.). How to Consolidate Your Student Loans — NerdWallet. NerdWallet. Retrieved June 17, 2023, from https://www.nerdwallet.com/article/loans/student-loans/consolidate-student-loans

Hintze, R. (2018, March 29). Pros and Cons: Should My Teen Work During High School? Student-Tutor Education Blog. https://student-tutor.com/blog/should-my-teen-work-during-high-school/

Hoffower, H. (2020, December 27). 17 things millionaires do differently from everyone else. Business Insider. https://www.businessinsider.com/millionaire-habits-how-to-build-wealth-time-energy-money-2019-4#they-invest-in-low-cost-index-funds-7

Home Owner. (n.d.). 9 Types of Personal Budgets. Homeowner. Retrieved May 18, 2023, from https://www.homeowner.com/personal-finance/types-of-personal-budgets

Hood, B. (2021, August 3). How to Avoid Five Common Financial Scams. Suits Me®. https://suitsmecard.com/blog/5-common-financial-scams-and-how-to-avoid-them

How To Find a Job as a Teenager (Plus Benefits and Job Types). (2023, January 30). Indeed Career Guide. https://www.indeed.com/career-advice/finding-a-job/how-to-find-job-as-teenager

Huffpost. (2019, March 25). 6 Apps Teens Can Use To Manage Money. HuffPost. https://www.huffpost.com/entry/money-apps-for-teens-and-parents_l_5c979128e4b01ebeef108c34

Hunt, M. (2023, May 31). Types Of Student Loans. Bankrate. https://www.bankrate.com/loans/student-loans/types-of-student-loans/#best

Iciciprulife. (n.d.). What is Life Insurance - Life Insurance Definition & Meaning | ICICI Prulife. Retrieved June 26, 2023, from https://www.iciciprulife.com/insurance-library/insurance-basics/what-is-life-insurance.html

Income Tax - Why Do We Pay Federal Income Tax. (2021, May 19). H&R Block. https://www.hrblock.com/tax-center/income/other-income/income-tax/

Indeed Editorial Team. (2020, January 3). 10 Benefits of Doing an Internship. Indeed

Career Guide. https://www.indeed.com/career-advice/career-development/bene
fits-of-internships

Investopedia. (2019). Simplified Employee Pension (SEP) Definition. Investopedia.
https://www.investopedia.com/terms/s/sep.asp

IRS. (n.d.-a). Publication 501 (2019), Dependents, Standard Deduction, and Filing
Information | Internal Revenue Service. Www.irs.gov. Retrieved May 8, 2023,
from https://www.irs.gov/publications/p501

IRS. (n.d.-b). Who Should File a Tax Return | Internal Revenue Service. Www.irs.gov.
Retrieved May 14, 2023, from https://www.irs.gov/filing/individuals/who-
should-file

IRS. (2018). Definition of Adjusted Gross Income | Internal Revenue Service. Irs.gov.
https://www.irs.gov/e-file-providers/definition-of-adjusted-gross-income

IRS. (2019a). Free File: Do Your Federal Taxes for Free | Internal Revenue Service.
Irs.gov. https://www.irs.gov/filing/free-file-do-your-federal-taxes-for-free

IRS. (2019b). Independent Contractor Self Employed or Employee | Internal Revenue
Service. Irs.gov. https://www.irs.gov/businesses/small-businesses-self-employed/
independent-contractor-self-employed-or-employee

IRS. (2019c). Topic No. 310 Coverdell Education Savings Accounts | Internal Revenue
Service. Irs.gov. https://www.irs.gov/taxtopics/tc310

JavaTPoint. (n.d.). Advantages and Disadvantages of Online Banking - Javatpoint.
Javatpoint. Retrieved June 10, 2023, from https://www.javatpoint.com/advan
tages-and-disadvantages-of-online-banking

Jayakumar, A. (2020, February 25). What's Your Money Personality? Take Our Quiz
to Find Out. NerdWallet. https://www.nerdwallet.com/article/finance/money-
personality

Kagan, J. (n.d.-a). Renewable Term Definition. Investopedia. Retrieved June 27, 2023,
from https://www.investopedia.com/terms/r/renewableterm.asp

Kagan, J. (n.d.-b). Why Overdraft Protection Matters. Investopedia. Retrieved June 9,
2023, from https://www.investopedia.com/terms/o/overdraft-protection.asp

Kagan, J. (2019a). 529 Plan. Investopedia. https://www.investopedia.com/terms/1/
529plan.asp

Kagan, J. (2019b). Amortized Loan Definition. Investopedia. https://www.investope
dia.com/terms/a/amortized_loan.asp

Kagan, J. (2019c). Income Tax Definition. Investopedia. https://www.investopedia.
com/terms/i/incometax.asp

Kagan, J. (2019d). *Taxable Income*. Investopedia. https://www.investopedia.com/terms/t/taxableincome.asp

Kagan, J. (2021, February 12). *How Companies use Revolving Loan Facilities*. Investopedia. https://www.investopedia.com/terms/r/revolving-loan-facility.asp

Kagan, J. (2022, January 3). *Individual Retirement Account (IRA)*. Investopedia. https://www.investopedia.com/terms/i/ira.asp

Kantrowitz, M. (2022, November 10). *How to Pay for College*. Savingforcollege. https://www.savingforcollege.com/article/how-to-pay-for-college

Kenton, W. (2022, July 26). *Understanding Payments*. Investopedia. https://www.investopedia.com/terms/p/payment.asp

Kilroy, A. (2020, May 4). *How Does Life Insurance Work?* Forbes Advisor. https://www.forbes.com/advisor/life-insurance/how-it-works/

Kunsman, T. (2021, July 7). *Why You Need Multiple Streams of Income Starting Right Now*. Invested Wallet. https://investedwallet.com/multiple-streams-of-income/

Lake, R. (n.d.-a). *Greenlight Review Debit Card for Kids – Forbes Advisor*. Forbes Advisor. Retrieved May 28, 2023, from https://www.forbes.com/advisor/banking/greenlight-card-review/

Lake, R. (n.d.-b). *What to Know About Insuring Teen Drivers*. Investopedia. Retrieved June 24, 2023, from https://www.investopedia.com/car-insurance-for-teens-guide-5089172

Lake, R. (2022, January 2). *Want a Better Credit Score? Here's How to Get It*. Investopedia. https://www.investopedia.com/how-to-improve-your-credit-score-4590097

Lake, R. (2023, March 3). *Teens and Income Taxes*. Investopedia. https://www.investopedia.com/teens-and-income-taxes-7152618

Lane, R. (2021, July 8). *How to Get a Health Professions Student Loan*. NerdWallet. https://www.nerdwallet.com/article/loans/student-loans/health-professions-student-loan

LaPonsie, M. (2018, June 15). *5 Ways Convenience Is Killing Your Budget*. US News. https://money.usnews.com/money/personal-finance/saving-and-budgeting/articles/2018-06-15/5-ways-convenience-is-killing-your-budget

LaPonsie, M. (2023, February 9). *4 Benefits of Filing Taxes Early*. U.S.News. https://money.usnews.com/money/personal-finance/articles/the-benefits-of-filing-taxes-early

Lauren. (2023, January 13). *GoHenry review - the best pocket money app?* Money to the Masses. https://moneytothemasses.com/banking/gohenry-review-the-best-pocket-money-app

Learn About Being a Babysitter | Indeed.com. (2022, June 25). Indeed Career Guide. https://www.indeed.com/career-advice/careers/what-does-a-babysitter-do

Learn.org. (n.d.). What Is a Technical Institute? Learn.org. Retrieved June 14, 2023, from https://learn.org/articles/What_is_a_Technical_Institute.html

Lee, D. J. (2014, November 27). 10 Sneaky Online Shopping Tricks For Scoring Major Discounts. Forbes. https://www.forbes.com/sites/deborahlee/2014/11/27/10-sneaky-online-shopping-tricks-for-scoring-major-discounts/?sh=1d9ec45e110b

Lee, M. (2019). Fixed and Variable Rate Loans: Which Is Better? Investopedia. https://www.investopedia.com/ask/answers/07/fixed-variable.asp

Lewis, F. (2013, July 25). 6 Reasons Why Should Teenagers Start Working Earlier-Infographic. JobCluster Blog. https://www.jobcluster.com/blog/teenagers-should-start-working-earlier/

Loic, L. (2022, July 26). 5 Tips to Save Money on Your Online Subscriptions. MUO. https://www.makeuseof.com/tips-save-money-online-subscriptions/

Lustig, M. (2020). Understanding the Types of Federal Student Loans. US News & World Report; U.S. News & World Report. https://www.usnews.com/education/blogs/student-loan-ranger/articles/understanding-the-types-of-federal-student-loans-available

Maheshwari, R. (2023, March 10). Insurance: Definition, How It Works And Main Types of Policies. Forbes Advisor INDIA. https://www.forbes.com/advisor/in/insurance/what-is-insurance/

Mann (Silvermann), B. (2021, January 15). How To Read (and Understand) Your Bank Statement. The Smart Investor. https://thesmartinvestor.com/banking/guides-banking/understand-bank-statement/

Mbabazi, E. (2021, June 21). What is an Emergency Fund and Why You Need One. Money254. https://www.money254.co.ke/post/what-is-an-emergency-fund-and-why-you-need-one

McGurran, B. (n.d.). How to Start Investing: A Guide for Beginners. NerdWallet. Retrieved June 21, 2023, from https://www.nerdwallet.com/article/investing/how-to-start-investing

Meet 16 Teen Founders Who Are Building Big Businesses -- and Making Big Money. (2019, August 20). Entrepreneur. https://www.entrepreneur.com/leadership/meet-16-teen-founders-who-are-building-big-businesses/337852

Meny-Gibert, E. (2021, April 8). *5 questions to ask yourself before you borrow money.* Oval Blog. https://blog.ovalmoney.com/post/5-questions-to-ask-yourself-before-you-borrow-money/

Miranda, D. (2022, October 8). *1099 Vs. W-2 : What's The Difference? – Forbes Advisor.* Forbes Advisor. https://www.forbes.com/advisor/business/w2-vs-1099/

Money Mindset. (n.d.). *Consolidated Credit.* Retrieved April 26, 2023, from https://www.consolidatedcredit.org/money-mindset/

Money Mindset: How a Scarcity Mentality is Making You Poor. (2021, September 15). *Nairobi Garage.* https://nairobigarage.com/how-scarcity-money-mindset-is-making-you-poor/

Moody, J. (2020). *Hispanic Serving Institutions: What to Know.* US News & World Report; U.S. News & World Report. https://www.usnews.com/education/best-colleges/articles/hispanic-serving-institutions-what-to-know

Morah, C. (2021, June 13). *Evaluating your personal financial statement.* Investopedia. https://www.investopedia.com/articles/pf/08/evaluate-personal-financial-statement.asp

Morgan Cautero, R. (n.d.). *Is Your Costco Habit of Buying in Bulk Costing You? The Balance.* Retrieved May 29, 2023, from https://www.thebalancemoney.com/how-much-does-buying-in-bulk-save-you-4165997

Mydoh. (2021, October 21). *How to Help Your Teen Find a Job.* Mydoh. https://www.mydoh.ca/learn/blog/career/parents-guide-to-helping-your-teen-get-a-job/

National Academy of Social Insurance. (n.d.). *What is Social Security Disability Insurance?* National Academy of Social Insurance. Retrieved June 26, 2023, from https://www.nasi.org/learn/social-security/what-is-social-security-disability-insurance/

Neidel, C. (2023, May 1). *How to Save Money: 22 Proven Ways.* NerdWallet. https://www.google.com/url?q=https://www.nerdwallet.com/article/finance/how-to-save-money&sa=D&source=docs&ust=1688333066283904&usg=AOvVaw34NfHzZW3WwB-ie49SpcmM

Nemours TeensHealth. (n.d.). *Health Insurance Basics (for Teens) - Nemours Kidshealth.* Nemours TeensHealth. Retrieved June 24, 2023, from https://kidshealth.org/en/teens/insurance.html

Nova, A. (2019, July 20). *Many Americans who can't afford a $400 emergency blame debt.* CNBC. https://www.cnbc.com/2019/07/20/heres-why-so-many-americans-cant-handle-a-400-unexpected-expense.html

O'Connell, B. (2022, January 25). *What Are Options? Forbes Advisor. https://www. forbes.com/advisor/investing/what-are-options/*

O'Shea, A., & Coombes, A. (2018, April 30). *What Is a Roth IRA? How to Get Started - NerdWallet. NerdWallet; NerdWallet. https://www.nerdwallet.com/article/ investing/what-is-a-roth-ira*

O'Shea, A., & Taube, S. (2023, May 22). *Custodial Roth IRA: What It Is, and Why Your Kid Needs One. NerdWallet. https://www.nerdwallet.com/article/investing/ why-your-kid-needs-a-roth-ira#:~:text=After%20the%20Roth%20IRA%20has*

Orem, T. (n.d.). *12 Tips to Cut Your Tax Bill This Year. NerdWallet. Retrieved May 15, 2023, from https://www.nerdwallet.com/article/taxes/tips-save-taxes*

Parys, S. (2023, April 20). *2022-2023 Tax Brackets and Federal Income Tax Rates. NerdWallet. https://www.nerdwallet.com/article/taxes/federal-income-tax-brack ets#:~:text=There%20are%20seven%20federal%20income%20tax%20rates%3A% 2010%25%2C%2012*

Pedigree. (n.d.). *Pedigree. Retrieved June 26, 2023, from https://www.pedigree.in/ health-and-grooming/medical-care/5-major-benefits-of-buying-pet-insurance*

Picardo, E. (2019). *Investing Definition. Investopedia. https://www.investopedia.com/ terms/i/investing.asp*

Post, J. (2023, February 21). *15 Companies Founded by Amazing Young Entrepreneurs - businessnewsdaily.com. Business News Daily. https://www.busi nessnewsdaily.com/5051-young-entrepreneurs.html*

Practical Business Skills. (2023). *Payment Options. Www.practicalbusinessskills.com. https://www.practicalbusinessskills.com/managing-a-business/financial-manage ment/payment-options*

Principal. (2022, November 14). *8 ways you can save on taxes in 2023. Principal. https://www.principal.com/individuals/build-your-knowledge/8-ways-you-can- save-taxes-2023*

Pritchard, J. (n.d.). *Why Pay Off Loans Early? Savings and Peace of Mind. The Balance. Retrieved June 6, 2023, from https://www.thebalancemoney.com/pay- off-loans-315588*

QuadFi. (2022, August 25). *Why Having Multiple Streams of Income is Beneficial | QuadFi. Quadfi.com. https://quadfi.com/why-having-multiple-streams-of- income-is-beneficial/*

Raisin. (2021, July 6). *Interest Rates Explained by Raisin. Raisin. https://www.raisin. com/interest-rates-explained/*

Raj, M. (2022, February 24). What Is The Diderot Effect And How It Works. Melvin Raj. https://www.melvinraj.com/what-is-the-diderot-effect-and-how-it-works/

Ramsey Solutions. (2022a, October 19). What Is a Direct PLUS Loan? Ramsey Solutions. https://www.ramseysolutions.com/debt/what-is-a-direct-plus-loan

Ramsey Solutions. (2022b, December 9). 4 Most Common Types of Bank Accounts. Ramsey Solutions. https://www.ramseysolutions.com/banking/types-of-bank-accounts

Real Simple. (n.d.). 6 Ways to Save Money as a College Student. Real Simple. Retrieved June 15, 2023, from https://www.realsimple.com/work-life/money/saving/save-money-on-college

Reiszel, J. (2020, May 6). 5 Ways to Practice Good Spending Habits. HRCCU. https://www.hrccu.org/blog/good-spending-habits/

Reynolds, I. (2023, January 4). Facebook Net Worth 2023: (Meta Platforms) Revenue Assets. CA Knowledge. https://caknowledge.com/facebook-net-worth/#Facebook_Net_Worth

Rivelli, E. (n.d.). How Much Is Gap Insurance? Investopedia. Retrieved June 26, 2023, from https://www.investopedia.com/how-much-is-gap-insurance-7483730

Rodriguez , J. (2022, March 25). Citi Custom Cash Credit Card Review 2022: Competitive Rates and Cash Back. GOBankingRates. https://www.gobankingrates.com/reviews/citi-custom-cash-credit-card/

Rosanes, M. (2023, February 6). Disability insurance: What is it and how does it work? Insurance Business. https://www.insurancebusinessmag.com/us/guides/disability-insurance-what-is-it-and-how-does-it-work-435262.aspx

Rose, J. (2018, May 10). 50 "Lit" Ways to Make Money as a Teenager. Good Financial Cents®. https://www.goodfinancialcents.com/make-money-teenager/

Royal, J. (2022, February 4). Saving vs. investing: Here are the key differences for managing your money. Bankrate. https://www.bankrate.com/investing/saving-vs-investing/

Safe Search Kids. (2021, April 14). How to Help Your Teens With Their First Job Search. Safe Search. https://www.safesearchkids.com/how-to-help-your-teens-with-their-first-job-search/

Sarah. (2021, August 11). How To Make Money As A Teenager: 25 Lucrative Ways. Clever Girl Finance. https://www.clevergirlfinance.com/blog/how-to-make-money-as-a-teenager/

Scholarships.com. (n.d.-a). Grants - Scholarships.com. Scholarships.com. Retrieved June 15, 2023, from https://www.scholarships.com/financial-aid/grants/

Scholarships.com. (n.d.-b). State Sponsored Grants - Scholarships.com. Scholarships.com. Retrieved June 15, 2023, from https://www.scholarships.com/financial-aid/grants/state-sponsored-grants/#:~:text=State%2Dsponsored%20grants%20are%20awarded

Schwahn, L. (n.d.). How to Choose the Right Budget System. NerdWallet. Retrieved May 18, 2023, from https://www.nerdwallet.com/article/finance/how-to-choose-the-right-budget-system

Sharkey, S. (2023, March 6). How To Make Money As A Teenager: 36 Lucrative Ways. Clever Girl Finance. https://www.clevergirlfinance.com/how-to-make-money-as-a-teenager/

Shawbrook. (n.d.). 5 questions to ask yourself before borrowing money. Shawbrook. Retrieved June 6, 2023, from https://www.shawbrook.co.uk/direct/personal-loans/article/5-questions-to-ask-yourself-before-borrowing-money/

Shiundu, W. (2022, June 22). The 7 Types of Personal Budgets and How to Choose. Money254. https://www.money254.co.ke/post/the-7-types-of-personal-budgets-and-how-to-choose-money-management

Shopify. (2022, June 22). 8 Popular Payment Options for Merchants. Shopify. https://www.shopify.com/blog/payment-options

Stessman, E. (2022, August 17). Is Your Costco Habit of Buying in Bulk Costing You? The Balance. https://www.thebalancemoney.com/how-much-does-buying-in-bulk-save-you-4165997

Strohm, M. (2021, February 24). 5 Benefits Of Digital Banking In 2021. Forbes Advisor. https://www.forbes.com/advisor/banking/benefits-of-digital-banking/

Suknanan, J. (n.d.). What is the 4% rule and how can it help you save for retirement? CNBC. Retrieved June 20, 2023, from https://www.cnbc.com/select/what-is-the-4-percent-retirement-savings-rule/

Surbhi S. (2017, October 21). Difference Between Needs and Wants (with Comparison Chart) - Key Differences. Key Differences. https://keydifferences.com/difference-between-needs-and-wants.html

Take Charge America Team. (2017, July 18). Our 5 Favorite Quotes About Saving Money. Take Charge America. https://www.takechargeamerica.org/our-5-favorite-quotes-about-saving-money/

Tavin, A. (n.d.). 8 Tips To Help You Stick To Your Budget. OppLoans. Retrieved May 21, 2023, from https://www.opploans.com/oppu/articles/8-tips-to-help-you-stick-to-your-budget/

Taxes for Teens - A Beginner's Guide. (2021, January 3). The Official Blog of

TaxSlayer. https://www.taxslayer.com/blog/teen-filing-first-tax-return/

The balance. (n.d.). Amortization Calculator. The Balance. Retrieved June 7, 2023, from https://www.thebalancemoney.com/amortization-calculator-5115846

The Pros and Cons of Working While in College. (2018, January 10). UAGC | University of Arizona Global Campus. https://www.uagc.edu/blog/the-pros-and-cons-of-working-while-in-college

Tierney, S. (n.d.). How to Avoid Overdraft Fees. NerdWallet. Retrieved June 11, 2023, from https://www.nerdwallet.com/article/banking/avoid-overdraft-fees

Timmons, M. (2023, April 10). Gap Insurance: How Does it Work and Do I Need it? Value Penguin. https://www.valuepenguin.com/how-gap-auto-insurance-works

Treece, K. (2020, July 17). What Is Loan Amortization? Forbes Advisor. https://www.forbes.com/advisor/loans/what-is-loan-amortization/

Treece, K. (2021, October 14). Your Guide To Student Loan Consolidation. Forbes Advisor. https://www.forbes.com/advisor/student-loans/student-loan-consolidation/

Turner, T. (2023, February 3). 47+ Fascinating Financial Literacy Statistics in 2022. Annuity.org. https://www.annuity.org/financial-literacy/financial-literacy-statistics/

United States Department of Labor. (2019). Age Requirements | U.S. Department of Labor. Dol.gov. https://www.dol.gov/general/topic/youthlabor/agerequirements

University, N. (2019, December 8). What are the main advantages and disadvantages when working while studying? New Castle University. https://international-blogs.ncl.ac.uk/blog/what-are-the-main-advantages-and-disadvantages-when-working-while-studying

Us News. (2019). The Best Accredited Online Colleges of 2019 |. USNews. https://www.usnews.com/education/online-education

UW Credit Union. (n.d.). 10 Common Financial Scams | UW Credit Union Winter 2019. UW Credit Union. Retrieved June 23, 2023, from https://www.uwcu.org/online-banking/articles/10-scams/

VanSomeren, L. (2021a, February 2). 16 Types of Loans to Help You Make Necessary Purchases. Forbes Advisor. https://www.forbes.com/advisor/loans/types-of-loans/

VanSomeren, L. (2021b, July 21). 9 Benefits Of Good Credit And How It Can Help You Financially. Forbes Advisor. https://www.forbes.com/advisor/credit-score/benefits-of-good-credit/

Waters, S. (2021, July 27). Personal Goals That Work: 20 Examples to Get Started. Betterup. https://www.betterup.com/blog/personal-goals

What is Investment? Investment Meaning, Types, Objectives. (n.d.). Www.canarahsb-clife.com. Retrieved June 19, 2023, from https://www.canarahsbclife.com/blog/financial-planning/what-is-investment

What Teens Should Know About Good Debt & Bad Debt. (n.d.). Getschooled.com. Retrieved June 5, 2023, from https://getschooled.com/article/5785-good-debt-vs-bad-debt/

White, A. (2020, February 13). *Credit card debt in the U.S. hits all-time high of $930 billion—here's how to tackle yours with a balance transfer.* CNBC. https://www.cnbc.com/select/us-credit-card-debt-hits-all-time-high/

White, J., & Bottorff, C. (n.d.). *SimplyHired Review 2023: Features, Pricing & More – Forbes Advisor. Www.forbes.com.* Retrieved June 11, 2023, from https://www.forbes.com/advisor/business/simplyhired-review/

Whiteside, E. (2022, September 17). *What is the 50/20/30 budget rule?* Investopedia. https://www.investopedia.com/ask/answers/022916/what-502030-budget-rule.asp

Wohlfert, S. (2022a, April 1). *5 Tips for Helping Teens With Their First Job.* One Voice Magazine. https://onevoicebhm.org/5-tips-helping-teens-their-first-job

Wohlfert, S. (2022b, April 1). *5 Tips for Helping Teens With Their First Job.* One Voice Magazine. https://onevoicebhm.org/5-tips-helping-teens-their-first-job

Zambas, J. (2015, November 12). *Employment rights for young people.* Nidirect. https://www.nidirect.gov.uk/articles/employment-rights-young-people

Zambas, J. (2021, September 6). *12 Benefits of Working a Part-Time Job as a Student.* Careeraddict. https://www.careeraddict.com/5-benefits-for-students-who-work-part-time-jobs

Zanzalari, D. (2022, June 25). *Why You Absolutely Need To Invest.* The Balance. https://www.thebalancemoney.com/why-is-investing-important-5222360

Zimmer, E. (2023, May 10). *Best Debit Cards for Kids and Teens in May 2023: GoHenry, BusyKid and More.* CNET Money. https://www.cnet.com/personal-finance/credit-cards/best/debit-cards-for-kids-and-teens/#comparing-card-fees-and-age-restrictions

IMAGE REFERENCES

Baumeister, M. (2020). *white and black wooden quote board* [Unsplash.com]. https://unsplash.com/photos/Y_LgXwQEx2c

Danilyuk, P. (2021). *photo-of-fresh-graduates* [Pexels.com]. https://www.pexels.com/photo/photo-of-fresh-gradutes-7942437/

Grabowska, K. (2020a). *Board-on-top-of-cash-bills* [Pexels.com]. https://www.pexels.com/photo/quote-board-on-top-of-cash-bills-4386367/

Grabowska, K. (2020b). *woman-calculating-money-and-receipts-using-a-calculator* [Pexels.com]. https://www.pexels.com/photo/woman-calculating-money-and-receipts-using-a-calculator-5900228/

Miroshnichenko, T. (2021a). *close-up-shot-of-a-person-holding-a-tablet* [Pexels.com]. https://www.pexels.com/photo/close-up-shot-of-a-person-holding-a-tablet-6913327/

Miroshnichenko, T. (2021b). *hands-of-a-person-holding-a-smartphone* [Pexels.com]. https://www.pexels.com/photo/hands-of-a-person-holding-a-smartphone-6694952/

Monstera. (2020). *insurance-inscription-under-umbrella* [Pexels.com]. https://www.pexels.com/photo/cutout-paper-appliques-of-insurance-inscription-under-umbrella-5849552/

Prophsee Journals. (2019). *life is your creation card* [Unsplash.com]. https://unsplash.com/photos/sFTMwH2Tvec

Rosly, A. (2019). *Pen on you're capable of amazing things spiral notebook* [Unsplash.com]. https://unsplash.com/photos/6GZQo28ecoE

www.ingramcontent.com/pod-product-compliance
Lightning Source LLC
Chambersburg PA
CBHW071543210326
41597CB00019B/3096